INSIGHT INTO

ANXIETY

INSIGHT INTO

ANXIETY

Chris Ledger and Clare Blake

Copyright 2007 © CWR

Published 2007 by CWR, Waverley Abbey House, Waverley Lane, Farnham, Surrey GU9 8EP, UK. Registered Charity No. 294387. Registered Limited Company No. 19903080.

The rights of Chris Ledger and Clare Blake to be identified as the authors of this work have been asserted by them in accordance with the Copyright, Designs and Patents Act 1988, sections 77 and 78.

See back of book for list of National Distributors.

Unless otherwise indicated, all Scripture references are from the Holy Bible: New International Version (NIV), copyright © 1973, 1978, 1984 by the International Bible Society.
Other versions used:
Amplified: The Amplified Bible © 1987 Zondervan and the Lockman Foundation
The Message. Copyright © by Eugene H. Peterson, 1993, 1994, 1995, 1996, 2000, 2001, 2002. Used by permission of NavPress Publishing Group.
NRSV: New Revised Standard Version, © 1989, Division of Christian Education of the National Council of the Churches of Christ in the United States of America
Phillips: J.B. Phillips The New Testament in Modern English , © 1960, 1972, J.B. Phillips, Fount Paperbacks

Concept development, editing, design and production by CWR

Printed in England by CPD

ISBN: 978-1-85345-436-3

WAVERLEY ABBEY
INSIGHT SERIES

The Waverley Abbey Insight Series has been developed in response to the great need to help people understand and face some key issues that many of us struggle with today. CWR's ministry spans teaching, training and publishing, and this series draws on all of these areas of ministry.

Sourced from material first presented over Insight Days by CWR at their base, Waverley Abbey House, presenters and authors have worked in close co-operation to bring this series together, offering clear insight, teaching and help on a broad range of subjects and issues. Bringing biblical understanding and godly insight, these books are written both for those who help others and those who face these issues themselves.

CONTENTS

FOREWORD

If I were asked to describe modern society with one word, I could think of no better one than 'anxious'. We live in an 'anxious society' and so many lives are dominated by fear – fear of crime, of terrorism, of intrusion, of global warming and climate change, of asylum seekers and so on. And, in fact, every institution in society seems to be afflicted by a general climate of anxiety, including the Church. Christians fear decline, we fear growth, and we fear change.

In our individual lives there is so much overwork, stress and busyness that it's little wonder that we learn to experience fear and anxiety over apparently minor things. We are so concerned about image that even as we go about leisure activities we are bothered about how we look to others. In their careers, so many people are overburdened with expectations that they find it difficult to balance work with home life.

Even the pleasures of a family life are infected by varying degrees of panic about whether the children will get into the right school, or get the right exam results. In fact, facing the pressure of SATS our children and grandchildren are being exposed to anxiety and fear of failure at an earlier age than ever before.

Healthy fear teaches caution in the face of danger. Unhealthy anxiety can paralyse us and destroy lives.

It is little wonder then that so many people experience the symptoms of anxiety in both mild and extreme forms, including panic attacks, phobias, post-traumatic stress disorder and obsessive compulsive disorders.

Christine Ledger and Clare Blake have provided yet another excellent introduction into a contemporary problem in the

Waverley Abbey Insight Series with *Insight into Anxiety*. Christine certainly knows what she is talking about as an experienced counsellor, a Christian lay minister and a long-term carer for her daughter, Julia, who suffers from ME.

Consequently, this is not merely a clinical introduction to anxiety, nor a theoretical one, but a deeply practical and helpful overview of the subject. As well as providing a must-read account of the nature of anxiety, psychological understandings of the term, and descriptions of how it is experienced by so many people today, Christine and Clare offer very helpful steps on overcoming different symptoms of anxiety, including relaxation and breathing exercises, as well as more fundamental pointers towards reorientating one's life and learning to be at ease.

There are also theological insights aplenty as the authors identify a number of biblical texts that deal with 'anxiety'. The key lesson for the contemporary Christian is to remember that while the Bible admonishes us not to be anxious this is not to make us feel even worse about ourselves. The point is that by 'casting' our anxiety upon God we find security and refuge from even our deepest fears. This is a spiritual discipline which Christine and Clare ably combine with the practice of counselling.

Lady Eileen Carey

INTRODUCTION

This book has grown out of a seminar given by Chris Ledger at Waverley Abbey House and demonstrates Chris's deep concern for those whose lives are blighted by anxious feelings. Anxiety affects many people, whether mildly with a tendency to worry, or severely when it can seriously affect the quality of life of the person suffering. Chris explores the subject in depth, seeking to help us understand exactly what anxiety is, what causes it, and how we can manage our anxiety with the help of proven skills and strategies.

In these pages Chris draws on a rich fund of wisdom gained from her work as an experienced counsellor, her role as a licensed lay minister, and particularly her own very personal experience as a long-time carer for her daughter with ME, where Chris learned to hand her anxiety over to a loving God who, she discovered, was faithful in every circumstance.

Cast all your anxiety on him because he cares for you. (1 Pet. 5:7)

Clare Blake

NOTE FROM CHRIS LEDGER

Worry, fear and anxiety can be like a psychological poison causing great distress, as in releasing their deadly toxins they appear to contaminate our whole being. However, there are antidotes. The first is to find a greater security in our heavenly Father so that we can go to Him with childlike faith and trust

Him with difficulties that are beyond our control. Secondly, we can actually learn how to manage the restricting mental, behavioural and bodily symptoms of the anxiety response which can be so very distressing and frightening for sufferers. In many years of counselling experience, I have found working with very anxious clients one of the most rewarding areas because lives can be so tangibly changed.

The purpose of this book is to help you put your roots deeper into the soil of God's love, thus becoming more dependent upon Him, and to give you the skills to manage and control the distressing symptoms of anxiety – not only for yourself, but also as you try to understand and help others. Clare has done a fine job in taking my notes and creating a resourceful book which I hope and pray you will find helpful.

CHAPTER ONE

WHAT IS ANXIETY?

INTRODUCTION

> Anxiety is a thin stream of fear trickling through the mind. If encouraged,
> it cuts a channel into which all other thoughts are drained.
>
> Arthur Somers Roche

What words or pictures spring to mind when you hear the term
'anxiety'? Delegates at one of Chris' conferences came up with
some striking images:

Lots of twisted strands
A coiled string getting tighter
A furrowed brow
Running away

A quivering jelly
Out of control
Overwhelmed
Cast adrift
Tense
Help!
Vulnerable
Hopeless
Insecure
Wound up

The *Compact Oxford English Dictionary* tells us that anxiety is 'a concern about an imminent or future difficulty' [1] while the *Collins English Dictionary* describes it as 'distress of mind, apprehension, uneasiness, disquietude'.[2] Another particularly accurate description that Chris once heard is that anxiety is 'fear spread out thinly'.

Anxiety is rather like an octopus that enfolds us in a suffocating grasp that can be very hard to break and includes distressing conditions such as OCD (obsessive-compulsive disorder), phobias and panic attacks. Anxiety impacts both our physical and mental wellbeing causing heart trouble, high blood pressure, stomach disorders, irritable bowel syndrome, back and neck pain, migraine, headaches, fatigue, insomnia, depression, and many other conditions.

However, the good news is that anxiety can improve with the help of specific skills and strategies, and by placing our reliance on God. Anxious people can emerge from their distressing symptoms as they learn to manage their anxiety, rather than let their anxiety manage them.

ANXIETY IS A NORMAL RESPONSE

The first thing we must recognise is that anxiety is a normal part of the human experience. It is how God has made us, a natural response to what is going on around us, and healthy levels of anxiety are vital for our survival. It is the body's way of saying 'Pay attention to this – it could have consequences for you.'

Anxiety is very much a part of daily life – for example, a person just about to go on stage may complain of 'stage fright'– actually not a handicap but a benefit as 'stage fright' releases extra adrenalin into the system, enabling an energy-charged performance. Another example is the person just about to take an exam where the anxiety 'gears up' the body for the approaching task. Anxiety is also an essential response to an imminent or future difficulty or threat.

WHEN ANXIETY BECOMES A PROBLEM

However, anxiety becomes a problem when it is exaggerated or experienced out of context. In this scenario, anxiety may cause us to become irrational, and a cycle of distress may develop.

For example, if you were about to cross a road in front of a bus a certain amount of normal anxiety would ensure that you didn't get knocked down by it! However, if you were sitting in a park near a main road, and the presence of nearby buses made your anxiety levels rise steeply – 'Oh my goodness, there are buses there' – that would be a very abnormal response.

While a normal and healthy anxiety response protects us, unhealthy anxiety is exaggerated, irrational and causes cycles of distress to develop. It's a continuum, as demonstrated over the page, where the feeling we experience does not correspond to a real threat or appropriate response to a situation.

A CONTINUUM FOR HEALTHY AND UNHEALTHY ANXIETY

Healthy anxiety
(A real threat)
eg If I met a lion,
I would run for my life

Unhealthy anxiety
(A threat out of balance)
eg I avoid flying
because I am terrified
the plane will crash

> Tim (nineteen), had always been an anxious child – when visitors came he would hide his face in his mother's skirt and refuse to talk to them, and at school he was always very quiet. However, Tim now finds that whereas he used to feel anxious on specific occasions he now suffers from almost constant anxiety without any real reason. 'I worry about everything – my work at university, going out with friends, whether I've switched all the plugs off in my flat. University is meant to be fun, but I feel so anxious I can't enjoy anything – I am probably going to have to leave as I don't think I can cope any more.'

THE BIBLE AND ANXIETY

It's always good to look at Scripture as it has a surprising amount to say about the subject of anxiety. In Proverbs 12:25 we read, 'An anxious heart weighs a man down.' How many of us know that heavy dragging feeling only too well?

One of the most quoted verses on anxiety is Philippians 4:6: 'Do not be anxious about anything, but in everything, by prayer and petition, with thanksgiving, present your requests to God.' The trouble is that if we take the words 'Do not be anxious about anything' literally we can quickly get into a real guilt trip. Some people reading these words feel condemned – 'Oh my goodness, I am anxious. That makes me the world's worst person' – and as a result, may also feel that they are inferior Christians.

Our faulty human natures prevent us attaining the complete peace that every Christian aspires to, but God has made provision for this; 1 Peter 5:7 says, 'Cast all your anxiety on him because he cares for you' and this encapsulates the true essence of dealing with anxiety. It is about actually casting our anxiety upon God, trying to find God in the middle of it.

DAVID – AN ANXIOUS MAN?

David is described in the Old Testament as a man after God's own heart (see 1 Sam. 13:14), but he was also someone who demonstrated real anxiety at certain points of his eventful life.

David's life was a rollercoaster of ups and downs. As a young teenager he was plucked from the obscurity of tending sheep to be anointed king of Israel. However, the road to kingship for David was not straightforward, for once Saul heard the women singing after battle, 'Saul has slain his thousands, and David his tens of thousands' (1 Sam. 18:7), he did everything in his power to destroy his former favourite (1 Sam. 19–22).

As we read these chapters, we can see in David a number of typical anxious behaviours. One of the most common of these is to escape from anxiety-producing situations, and we see David doing this by distancing himself from the cause of his anxiety and running away to a sanctuary presided over by a priest called Ahimelech. So far, David had behaved in a very practical way, but at this point, like many anxiety sufferers, his fear caused him to behave in an irrational way.

David was so frightened for his life that he began to tell lies to the priest, saying that he was alone because he was performing an urgent errand for King Saul. In refusing to face up to the truth of the actual situation, instead acting in an irrational manner to cope with it, David reflects a typical behaviour for anxiety sufferers.

From then on, David's anxiety spiralled into even more irrational behaviour. Still not feeling safe, he fled further into the enemy country of Gath, but when the king of Gath's servants started repeating the women's victory song, 'Saul has slain his thousands and David his tens of thousands', David's anxiety about his life reached such a pitch that he feigned insanity. Completely overwhelmed by his fears, David exhibited yet another common anxiety behaviour as he withdrew totally from the threatening situation and escaped to the security of the cave of Adullam.

DAVID FINDS HELP FOR HIS ANXIETY

David's experience in this cave and the emotions he felt in hiding are clearly shown in the painfully honest and heartfelt words of Psalm 142:1–2: 'I cry aloud to the LORD; I lift up my voice to the LORD for mercy. I pour out my complaint before him; before him I tell my trouble.'

From this psalm it is easy to picture David's intensely anxious state of mind. He probably felt a strong sense of disillusionment, 'Oh God, it's not fair – you picked me out. I didn't ask to be anointed king, and now look what has happened – my life is in jeopardy.'

However, the psalm does not just brood on David's anxious state and, as you continue reading, you can see why God so loved this man. Although David was weak and fearful, he knew where to go for help, and at his lowest point he still held onto God. The key is verse 5: 'You are my refuge.' On the one hand David is struggling with his faulty humanity, but on the other hand he is rooting himself in God. He does not allow himself to be totally swamped by his negative feelings, but reminds himself of God's character and trusts in the relationship that he has with Him: 'You are my refuge.'

David shows us how to cope with anxiety in this and many other psalms, such as Psalm 77, that reveal genuine feelings of strong anxiety, but also show David's determination not to wallow and be overcome by them. He chooses instead to focus on God, and reminds us through his example that our anxiety can be dealt with if we stand firm in our security in God.

Yes, we will get anxious – that is part of the human condition – but we can find a way to stand in God. God is so great. He is our God, the God of the impossible, and He displays His power (Psa. 77:14). How can we doubt that He will help us in our anxiety?

WHAT IS ANXIETY?

Many people confuse anxiety with stress, but where the latter is more to do with our reactions to pressure, anxiety is a response to any issue we encounter that provokes a sense of fear within us. Anxiety raises questions like:

- Will I cope?
- Am I adequate?
- What will happen?
- Will it work out OK?

In its simplest form, anxiety is a response to a threat – *real or imagined* – and the first issue when trying to help a person with any anxiety problem is to explore their threat. Is it real, or is it imagined?

For instance, a woman could be facing a physical threat because her partner is an alcoholic who is sometimes abusive. This is a real threat and her fear relating to possible violence is a real anxiety. However, the anxiety could also be triggered by an imagined threat. The woman this time may be in a relationship where she constantly feels anxious about pleasing her partner, based on an underlying worry that her partner may reject her. This may or may not be true, but if not this woman's anxiety actually stems from an imagined threat.

However, whether real or imagined, both may equally result in increased anxiety levels. Anxiety then becomes a problem if the person feels unable to find a solution for their real or imagined threat which can lead to anxiety spiralling out of control, even though it may not be in proportion to the original circumstances or threat. Anxiety gives rise to 'What if?' questions. 'What if this happens, what if that happens, what if I cannot handle the situation?'

Michelle's fiancé wants them to have a luxurious honeymoon abroad, but Michelle can't face it because she is terrified of flying. Films and news reports, particularly the Twin Towers terrorist incident at the World Trade Center, New York, have convinced Michelle that if she were to be a passenger on a plane, something terrible would happen. She cannot stop saying to herself, 'What if the plane crashes? I will die.' Her fiancé cannot really understand the way she feels, and it has been causing a lot of tension between them.

ANXIETY FEELINGS

Anxiety can take many forms. Often the feelings involve:

- a deep uncertainty about the future
- questions like: 'What will happen?' 'Will I be able to cope?'
- an overwhelming sense of panic
- an inner awareness of shame
- vague but very real sense of being worried (GAD – generalised anxiety disorder)
- very specific fear (phobia).

Anxiety can be an immensely strong feeling. Have you ever experienced high levels of anxiety as you really, really hoped that you would not be the one chosen for something that you didn't want to do? In such a situation your heart thumps as though it is going to explode, your body feels very tense, and maybe your palms get hot and sweaty – anybody else please – just not me! These bodily symptoms are caused by anxiety.

When you begin to give attention to anxious thoughts like, 'Oh my goodness, can I do this? What's going to happen? How embarrassed I am. Will people reject me? Will they think I'm silly?' it triggers off a biochemical function in the brain, giving rise to physical symptoms. To put it simply, you feel your anxiety in your body.

ANXIETY AND THE CWR WHOLENESS MODEL

However, anxiety affects far more than just the physical area, as we will see if we look at the CWR Wholeness Model which illustrates the five areas that our anxiety may affect.

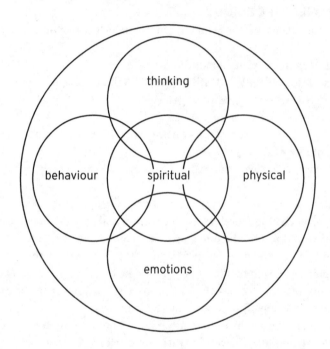

THE CWR WHOLENESS MODEL

God created us as whole beings with every area interconnecting, and anxiety affects each area in different yet related ways.

- Physical area – bodily symptoms
- Emotional area – emotions: worry, apprehension, fear, anticipation
- Thinking area – irrational thoughts causing psychological changes
- Behavioural area – choosing to avoid or increase anxiety
- Spiritual area – meeting our deep spiritual needs in God

Anxiety impacts the physical area causing unpleasant symptoms in our body, while in the emotional area we may experience a wide variety of emotions in addition to the anxiety, including confusion, feeling out of control etc.

Thirdly, anxiety affects our thinking level where our thoughts can actually make the anxiety more overwhelming and more intense. For example, if we were to stand up to speak in front of an audience and think 'I can't cope with this – they are all looking at me. I know I will run out of words, and do a terrible job. This is awful. Why on earth am I here? What if they don't like me?' our anxiety would steadily rise.

Actual spoken words average around 500 words a minute, but the self-talk going on in the subconscious mind averages a staggering 1,500 words a minute. So if we feed our minds with negative thoughts such as 'I can't cope, this is awful …' there is no doubt that we will end up feeling anxious.

Another area affected by anxiety is our actual behaviour. One of the most important factors in anxiety, and the reason that it often continues to be a problem, is that the common response to anxiety is to avoid the situation that creates it. Sadly, such avoidance nurtures the anxiety rather than dealing with it.

Finally, we need to evaluate how well we are meeting our deep spiritual needs in God in the presence of anxiety. What happens to our relationship with God? Are we able to trust Him? Anxiety can have a strong impact in this area also, and it is vital for our wholeness that we learn to anchor ourselves in God however we are feeling.

Luke was doing well in his job until his first presentation. He had always been clumsy and a number of things went wrong owing to nerves – he spilled some coffee, got some of the slides mixed up, and when questions were asked he couldn't answer all of them. His boss said it was all part of the learning curve, but Luke now finds that whenever he knows he has to give a talk in front of other people he gets very anxious, with his internal talk saying, 'I can't do this. I know I am going to dry up and I will lose my job.' He feels dizzy, stammers, finds that his mind goes blank, and often ends up with a migraine. Luke's anxiety has got so bad that he has even rung in sick on a few occasions. Although initially quite sympathetic, his boss is now telling Luke that he must snap out of it, which just makes him even more anxious.

AN ALTERNATIVE ANXIETY MODEL

Another useful way to identify how anxiety affects us is to write the word 'Anxiety' in the middle of a piece of paper, and then write down how it affects the different areas of our life, as illustrated in the diagram opposite.

For example, symptoms might include hyper-vigilance where

people simply can't shut their thoughts off so that their anxiety runs round and round in their head like a hamster in a ball, or poor concentration where the sufferer spends so much time trying to deal with the anxiety that it is impossible to focus on anything else.

Writing your own individual experience in this way – how anxiety affects *you* – is a helpful way to view your anxiety objectively.

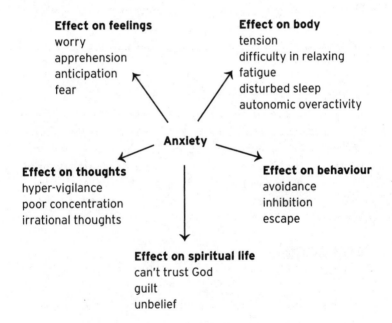

Effect on feelings
worry
apprehension
anticipation
fear

Effect on body
tension
difficulty in relaxing
fatigue
disturbed sleep
autonomic overactivity

Anxiety

Effect on thoughts
hyper-vigilance
poor concentration
irrational thoughts

Effect on behaviour
avoidance
inhibition
escape

Effect on spiritual life
can't trust God
guilt
unbelief

ACTIVITY

Think of a situation or an event that has given you a high level of anxiety, and use either the CWR Wholeness Model or the Alternative Anxiety Model to look at it from an objective perspective, examining what you experienced in the different areas. Ask yourself questions such as: 'What were my thoughts at this point?' 'How did anxiety affect my behaviour?' Think carefully, explore your anxiety, and see where it produced the greatest effect, writing in as much detail as you can.

My event _____ (eg going to meet new people)

_____

_____

How do you feel when you see this information set out on paper? Does it help you see the big picture? This is a really helpful technique as it is not only releasing for the person with the anxiety, but is also a very constructive tool for those trying to help others, as they can then identify specific issues by looking at what has been revealed, and ask 'What's going on here? What areas need addressing?'

REFLECTION

Focus on the following verses:

He who dwells in the shelter of the Most High will rest in the shadow of the Almighty. I will say of the LORD, 'He is my refuge and my fortress, my God, in whom I trust.' … 'Because he loves me,' says the

LORD, 'I will rescue him; I will protect him, for he acknowledges my name. He will call upon me and I will answer him; I will be with him in trouble, I will deliver him and honour him.'

Psa. 91:1–2,14–15

- Think about what it means to dwell in the shelter of the Most High – how does that make you feel?
- Meditate for a few minutes on these words: rest, refuge, fortress.
- How does the Lord respond when we are in trouble? What sort of things does He do?
- Think of a time or times when God has been a refuge to you. If you cannot personally remember such a time, look at the Bible for inspiration, eg Ruth, David, Joseph, or the lives of Christian pioneers such as Hudson Taylor and Mother Teresa.

PRAYER

Father God,

Sometimes I just need to know that You are here for me. Thank You that I know that when I call to You, You are never too busy to hear me, and that You always respond. It helps me feel stronger just to know that You promise to be with me whatever happens if I call on Your name. Thank You that even though I don't always understand some of the things that I am going through, I will hold on to the fact that You say that You will be with me – I couldn't wish for anything better. Thank You that when I feel anxious and alone, You promise to provide a shelter for me where I can rest in You. Help me to really let that truth sink into me. Amen.

CHAPTER TWO

WHO IS VULNERABLE TO ANXIETY?

INTRODUCTION

Worry often gives a small thing a big shadow.

Anon

Some people seem to be more vulnerable to feeling anxious than others, and significant life events may also deeply affect anxiety levels. Such events can be any sort of trauma where we have been emotionally, physically or sexually abused; car accidents, terrorist experiences, illness or death, or things we are taught in childhood (eg if you are naughty the police will take you away), and challenging experiences, eg giving a public talk, having a new baby, redundancy.

PERSONALITIES SUSCEPTIBLE TO ANXIETY

Research has clearly shown that some types of personality are much more susceptible to anxiety than others. Many anxiety sufferers have what psychologists describe as type A personalities, naturally driven perfectionists predisposed towards anxiety because perfectionism is nearly always partnered by a fear of failure. On the other hand, shy and withdrawn people will also often become anxious because they have never learnt to be assertive and if they say 'no' they fear rejection.

A DYSFUNCTIONAL FAMILY

Another common factor is family history. Growing up in an atmosphere where negative messages pollute the home, or where a parent suffers with a Generalised Anxiety Disorder (GAD) can leave a child thinking it is normal to be anxious.

Such an upbringing is rather like growing up in a fairground Hall of Mirrors. Year after year you are presented with a distorted image of yourself with big head and little bowed legs until finally you come to believe it, and not even a glimpse of yourself as you actually are in an ordinary mirror can convince you otherwise.

This is just what can happen to those unfortunate enough to grow up in a family where the message that you are 'no good' is constantly reflected back day after day. With the constant refrain 'I am no good because I have been told I'm no good. I can't do this. I can't possibly do that', troubling their mind, it is no wonder that they have problems with confidence and find anxiety levels hit the ceiling when asked to undertake a task such as speaking at a conference.

Ruth grew up in a family where her mother was afraid of many things – thunderstorms, the dark, spiders, meeting new people. Ruth found herself in adulthood wanting to break free from what she could see was an inherited anxious state of mind where she couldn't sleep unless the bedside lamp was on, and worried every time she saw a spider's web in case a spider lurked nearby. Her mother had also constantly fed her negative messages, and when Ruth wanted to become a journalist discouraged her with statements like: 'You'll never be able to do that – you're far too shy.' Ruth had tried to break free of the anxious patterns of her childhood, but they were very strong and whenever she was under pressure she found that her anxiety would take over her life and make her feel unable to cope.

OTHER ANXIETY FACTORS

Another factor in anxiety is a psychologically biased thinking style, as we will discover in Chapter Three. Stressful circumstances also play a significant role, especially if several life stresses occur together because anxiety is a common by-product of stress. The amount of anxiety we experience is also partly dependent on how well developed our coping skills are – again often linked to our personality type. Another contributory factor is the presence or absence of a good social support system as, if we lack that vital network of family and/or friends, our anxiety levels often increase sharply.

COMMON SOURCES OF ANXIETY

There are many different issues that can cause us anxiety and these often vary according to our stage in life – for example, as we get older, health may become a major cause of anxiety, whereas for younger people lack of finance may head the list. The following list contains some of the most common anxiety factors, and obviously a combination of two or more may greatly increase anxiety levels, eg a husband losing his job and a wife becoming pregnant.

- Health
- Your children
- Your job
- Relationships
- Pregnancy
- Promotion
- Growing old
- Domestic upheaval
- Financial problems
- Legal difficulties
- Exams

IDENTIFYING THE THREAT

As already stated, anxiety is always a response to a threat, and how high our anxiety rises depends on how we perceive that threat. There are three major types of anxiety based on three types of threat. The first one is the objective real threat, the second the subjective assessed threat, and the third is threats to expectations and self-image.

THE OBJECTIVE REAL THREAT

The objective real threat is a very concrete form of threat – for instance, a firefighter must handle his fear of fire to perform his job properly. A more personal example of an objective real threat was experienced when Chris's anxiety levels soared as never before during a trip to Florida.

The threat came from a surprising source – not the alligators in the Alligator Park where she and her husband were enjoying a relaxed picnic, but a squirrel that suddenly appeared beside their table, screaming and frothing at the mouth. Chris's immediate thought was rabies!

Her anxiety shot sky high – no way did she want to get rabies – and when the squirrel actually jumped onto the table, Chris didn't wait to see what would happen next, running away as fast as she could without even stopping to grab her lunch. In this case her anxiety was a valid response to a very objective real threat – the possibility that the squirrel might have rabies.

THE SUBJECTIVE ASSESSED THREAT (PHOBIAS)

However, the anxiety that prompted Chris's escape from this real threat might then have become distorted into anxiety caused by a subjective assessed threat (phobias). For instance, if she had a personality prone to anxiety this experience might then prompt a continuing irrational anxious response every time she saw a squirrel: 'Rabies, I must run.'

This is the essence of the subjective assessed threat. We become irrational about what might threaten us, and then these irrational anxious thoughts can escalate to become phobias. A phobia (derived from a Greek word meaning 'fearing') is considered to be an 'irrational fear' because no objective threat is involved.

In the case of phobias, anxiety levels rise steeply, and the nature of the response is illogical, leading many people who have become phobic to think they are going crazy, whereas the real problem is simply that the phobia causes strange reactions in the body and in the mind.

Unfortunately, people who are phobic can find it very difficult to share what they are experiencing as they often feel ashamed because they actually recognise that their response is irrational, but it is nonetheless intensely real for them and causes great distress.

THREATS TO EXPECTATIONS AND SELF-IMAGE

Threats to our expectations and self-image can come from a huge variety of sources, for anxiety can be caused by:

- possible promotion
- playing a game of golf
- position in class
- letting parents down
- husband's lack of affection
- having a less smart home than friends/family
- trying to ask a girl for a date
- lack of physical attraction
- fear of making a fool of oneself in public
- making love (performance anxiety)
- visiting parents-in-law
- negotiating deals
- wondering what the neighbours think.

ACTIVITY

Do you relate to any of these causes of anxiety, or perhaps others personal to you? What things do you get anxious about? Score each item for the highest level it reaches, eg 8/10.

_____

_____

_____

EXPECTATIONS AND ANXIETY

However, if you look more closely at the list you will note that none of them actually poses an objective threat to survival. The threat that they pose is a threat to self-image, and this is the basis for many people's anxiety as they see a situation threatening a high level of expectation of themselves – the more important the expectation, the more serious the threat, and the greater the likelihood of anxiety.

Because such anxiety is a response to a perceived threat, it often triggers the 'fight or flight' mechanism which allows us to escape any situation that causes anxiety and might cast doubt on our self-image. However, this response generally maintains and strengthens our anxious feelings, causing strong emotional and physical reactions which can result in disturbances in our thinking, disturbances in our behaviour, and can ultimately affect our relationship with God.

Lucy, aged thirty-four, was a late developer who had left school early without many qualifications. After working for a while she went to evening classes, studied hard, and got a place to study psychology at degree level. However, Lucy was very aware of how much older she was than the other students. She felt boring and unattractive, and found it particularly hard when her limited computer skills caused considerable amusement amongst her fellow students.

Although the degree was something that she really wanted to do, Lucy found it harder and harder to go into the university as she was convinced that the lecturers and the other students all thought she was wasting her time. She was particularly anxious about the spoken presentations, and was beginning to suffer from a mild level of panic attack, which was growing increasingly stronger. She was constantly fatigued and kept crying at the least thing which made her worry that she might be heading for a nervous breakdown.

ANXIETY AND OUR SPIRITUAL BEING

God has created us with deep spiritual needs: the need to feel a love which gives us a sense of security; a love which brings self-worth, and a love which gives us purpose in life. Anxiety arises when these spiritual needs are not being met in the appropriate way.

Jeremiah said, 'My people have committed two sins: They have forsaken me, the spring of living water, and have dug their own cisterns, broken cisterns that cannot hold water' (Jer. 2:13). We also often have broken cisterns because we try to meet our deep spiritual needs through pursuing inappropriate goals. It is when our goals become uncertain that anxiety arises.

Mark was very anxious because he was facing the uncertainty of his business folding. His goal had always been to have enough money to play and live well, and he now struggled to trust God for his future, because for him a future without money was bleak. He had not grown enough as a Christian to find his deep spiritual need for security met in God – he was digging a broken cistern. As a result, Mark felt very anxious about his future.

Of course there is nothing wrong in the idea of a goal in itself, as we all respond in one way or another to goals which we or others set – and God Himself had a goal to create the earth and to rescue us from the penalty of sin through Jesus Christ.

However, goals can become a problem when they take over our lives, or if they are set in concrete and are not flexible enough. If we look at our goals instead of looking at our goal in God, we will quickly run into problems.

Throughout his life the only way Jack could get his mother's attention was by doing well at school. However, the buzz he got from her delight at his achievements soon developed into a strongly perfectionist trait: 'When I am really good, my mother esteems me.'

So Jack got his sense of worth from that, and drove himself harder and harder, a habit that became part of his personality. Even as an adult, at root Jack's subconscious desire remained exactly the same – he drove himself to please his mother.

This was fine while he was getting plenty of business contracts and promotions, but then all of a sudden he hit a brick wall. His current boss didn't like him, and whatever Jack did seemed to be wrong, causing Jack's sense of worth to hit rock bottom, and anxiety to rise. The problem was that Jack could only get his self-worth when receiving affirmation through achieving his hidden goal – the praise and attention of his mother for his good work.

HIDDEN GOALS

We all have hidden goals, and to work out whether these are positive or negative we must ask certain questions: 'When I work towards my goal, where am I getting my sense of security, my sense of self-worth, and my sense of significance? Where and what do I look towards in my life for that?'

In common with many women, Chris's hidden goal was the need to be accepted, a need rooted in her childhood where she grew up in the shadow of a dominant twin sister. Her sister was the lively one, and got all the attention, so Chris's worth came to depend upon pleasing others in order to be accepted: 'When I am accepted I am worth something. When people like me I feel better about myself.'

Every hidden goal raises issues that we need to confront directly by asking ourselves some important questions.

- Who am I trying to please?
- Why do I drive myself in this way?
- Do I behave like this to receive esteem?
- Do I want to be recognised?

- Does my hidden goal become a problem because I am neglecting my relationship with God?
- What is my motivation?
- What do I expect to get out of this?

ACTIVITY

What is your hidden goal? What do you strive for? Identifying this is often extremely illuminating and will help you understand why you behave as you do. Write it down to help clarify your thoughts.

_____

_____

HIDDEN BELIEFS

Similarly we can also have hidden beliefs about ourselves that we may not even be conscious of, but nevertheless may be a powerful driving force beneath the surface.

For many people their hidden beliefs have reinforced feelings of worthlessness: 'I am no good. I am stupid. I am powerless.' Chris herself has found that when life gets difficult her hidden belief that she is inadequate, arising from her childhood feelings of being overshadowed by her sister, will rear its ugly head. However, she has learned to challenge this belief, and not to listen when the voice of her inner child reacts and says, 'I am inadequate.'

If we struggle with negative hidden beliefs, we also must challenge them and ask: 'Whose voice am I listening to? Is it the real me or just buried attitudes from the past or a parent's voice?

Who says I am unlovable?' Look at the facts and decide whether the belief you hold about yourself is true or not. If it is not, reject it.

Because Jane grew up in a family that had never affirmed her or encouraged her, the only way Jane could make sense of this neglectful attitude was to rationalise it by believing that the reason for her parents' behaviour was that she was unlovable.

For Jane 'I am unlovable' was a belief so deeply rooted in her mind that she really struggled with the idea that people might actually like her, and this made her anxious when she was with her friends. Sadly, her hidden continual belief, 'I am unlovable and people reject me because I am unlovable', reinforced feelings of rejection. For Jane the challenge was to move to a place where she could confront the 'I'm unlovable' belief and understand her worth in God's eyes.

ACTIVITY

Can you identify a hidden belief about yourself that causes you to become anxious?

_____

_____

_____

ANXIETY AND GOALS

So why does anxiety arise in relation to goals? The answer lies in our ability to achieve that goal, rather than in the pursuit of the goal in itself. We are fine if the goal is within our reach, but if it is not and appears uncertain, we can get very anxious, especially if our hidden belief is dependent upon that goal.

If the foundation for my self-worth rests on the belief that I must always be accepted and valued, or that I must always be clever, then when I fail to achieve these inflexible goals I will become very anxious. Also, such goals create problems because God made us to have our inner needs met in Him, and not in anything else.

However, having the right goal is important for us as we see in Philippians 3:13b–14: 'But one thing I do: Forgetting what is behind and straining towards what is ahead, I press on towards the goal to win the prize for which God has called me heavenwards in Christ Jesus.' There can be no better goal than the goal of pressing on with God.

SECURITY IN GOD

In order to cope with the uncertainties in life without our anxieties hitting the ceiling, it's important we focus our attention on learning how to meet our needs in God. When we are able to look to God and know that He is our Father and we are His children, we have an immense sense of security because He is always there for us. 'GOD, your God, is with you every step you take' (Josh. 1:9, *The Message*). How reassuring to know that He is always with us, and that we are secure in His arms (Deut. 33:27) – whatever happens.

God showed how important we are to Him by sending His beloved Son Jesus to die for us. Have you really understood this incredible truth? We are worth Jesus dying for us! That puts us in a totally secure place.

Again we can find our significance in God as Ephesians 2:10 reminds us that we are significant, and have been created to do good works. When we focus on that and find our anchorage in God, it helps lessen our anxiety and brings us peace.

WORKING TOWARDS MORE FLEXIBLE GOALS

A major part of dealing with anxiety is to make our goals more flexible. If our goal is set in concrete it is more likely to increase our anxiety, particularly if that goal is uncertain. The use of words such as 'should', 'ought' and 'must' are unhelpful because they make demands of oneself or others in an unhealthy way.

For example, if your goal were to give a good presentation and you were constantly saying to yourself, 'It *must* be OK, I *must* do a good job', you demand something of yourself that you may not be able to deliver, for your presentation may be far from perfect and you may stumble over your words (after all, we are fallible human beings!). As a result, your anxiety may rocket sky-high because you are anxious about attaining your concrete goal.

However, if your goal were more flexible and you were able to say to yourself, 'Well, I will do as good a job as I can, for my best is good enough', if it then all goes wrong, you can reassure yourself, 'Well, I did my best, and God knows what I am about' and your anxiety levels will be far less.

We can also put high demands upon others by saying, 'They *should* do this or they *ought* to do that' and if it's not done as we think it should be, we can become anxious. But who says they *should* or they *ought*? Our anxiety would be much lower if we were able to say to ourselves, 'It would be preferable if they did this, but if they don't, it's not the end of the world. God can still work in this situation.'

To summarise: to effectively counter the anxiety produced when our goal is not met, we need a flexible goal, or best of all, to have as our goal the aim of meeting our deepest needs in God.

To find out whether our goals will succeed in quenching our deep spiritual thirst for security and self-worth it's helpful to ask the following questions:

1. How rigid is that goal?
2. Will I reach that goal?
3. How important is that goal?
4. Where is God in that goal?

For Chris, her original goal of needing acceptance made her into a 'Yes' girl, the good girl in the class. She was afraid to disagree and her anxiety about whether people liked her or would reject what she had to offer made her an insecure person. Her inner belief was: 'I am inadequate.'

However, now Chris's goal is set on finding her security in God her belief is based on statements such as: 'I am of equal value and worth in God.' Whenever Chris finds herself getting anxious, she affirms her new belief and thinks, 'Well, what's my goal? Why is it uncertain? Where is God? How can I actually look to God in this and find my security in Him?' She has learned to be assertive and has found her voice.

ACTIVITY
Think of an event or person you feel anxious about and answer the following questions:

1. What is my goal?

_____

2. Why does it become uncertain (thereby increasing my anxiety)?

_____

3. What is my belief about myself?

_____

See if you can fit it together as a picture, as a concept. Try to make sense of what you have discovered about yourself and how this relates to your anxiety. Can your goal become more flexible? Where is God? Perhaps He feels far away – how can you bring Him into the situation?

REFLECTION

While you may have been telling yourself that you are worthless, this is not what the Bible says about those who love God. There are many verses that tell us how God sees us. Here are a few to begin with:

- I am a child of God: John 1:12
- I am Christ's friend: John 15:15
- I am a child of God, I can call Him my Father (Daddy!): Romans 8:14–15
- I am a temple for God's Holy Spirit living in me: 1 Corinthians 3:16

- I am a new person with my old life left behind:
  2 Corinthians 5:17
- I am hidden with Christ in God: Colossians 3:3

This is who you are in Christ. Read the list out loud and then choose one or two verses to memorise and use them next time you feel anxious. Think about Christ's death on the cross. What does that say about the way He feels about you? Do you still think you are worthless?

PRAYER

Father, please help me not to look in all the wrong places to get my sense of self-worth and significance. Help me to look to You instead and find my identity in You. When I think that Jesus died on the cross for me, it makes me realise how much You love me and that in Your eyes I am very precious. Help me to remember next time I am tempted to be overcome by a sense of worthlessness that I am Your child and a member of Your family. You love me and You say that I am a Somebody, not a Nobody. That makes me feel so cherished.

Thank You, Lord.

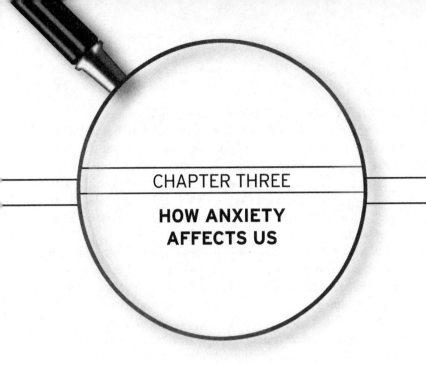

CHAPTER THREE

HOW ANXIETY AFFECTS US

INTRODUCTION

> When I look back on all these worries, I remember the story of the
> old man on his deathbed who said that he had had a lot of trouble in
> his life, most of which never happened.
>
> Winston Churchill

Anxiety affects us in a number of different ways – physically in
our bodies through the 'fight or flight' response with distressing
symptoms such as sweating, feeling sick etc, in our thinking
where we may experience irrational thoughts, and in our
behaviour as we try to avoid or escape the anxiety. Looking at
how anxiety affects us not only helps us understand what is going
on during anxious times, but gives us essential information on
how to manage it.

ANXIETY AND OUR SPIRITUAL LIFE

Our spiritual life is affected when we become anxious. On the one hand, we are professing faith in God and yet at the same time, we cannot seem to grasp the truth of His promises, a real dilemma that has a knock-on effect on our relationship with God. It's difficult to trust God when we are anxious and we can end up feeling so guilty about our anxiety that we start to believe that we don't deserve His blessings.

Worriers distrust God, and because their mind is not at peace, it is difficult to pray and spend time in deepening their relationship with God. Anxiety can also damage the temple of the Holy Spirit – 'Don't you know that you yourselves are God's temple and that God's Spirit lives in you?' (1 Cor. 3:16).

Anxiety sufferers need to learn to stand not on how they feel, but on what God has actually said about them: 'O afflicted one, storm-tossed, and not comforted, I am about to set your stones in antimony and lay your foundations with sapphires' (Isa. 54:11, NRSV).

ANXIETY AND OUR BODIES
PHYSIOLOGICAL CHANGES

One reason why anxiety is so feared by people is that it can have immense physical power. We hear people say things like, 'I felt sick with worry' or 'I was so nervous my hands were shaking'. This is because an emotional arousal of anxiety is triggered by an unconscious biochemical reaction from our autonomic nervous system (ANS).

The ANS regulates both the sympathetic and parasympathetic nervous systems which work in contrasting ways. The sympathetic nervous system releases adrenalin which gears us up for 'fight or flight' and charges our body up to run, while the parasympathetic nervous system slows our body down to rest.

So if you are someone who has become highly charged, and your sympathetic nervous system is working overtime releasing lots of adrenalin and causing you high levels of anxiety, an effective way of bringing the anxiety down again is to learn how to activate the parasympathetic nervous system by using breathing exercises and relaxation (see Chapter Five).

It is the sympathetic nervous system that is automatically triggered if a person unexpectedly encounters a lion in the garden. Immediately, the brain perceives a dangerous threat to life, causing adrenalin to be released into the body and resulting in a burst of extra energy so that the threatened person can run much faster than normal to escape the danger.

THE 'FIGHT OR FLIGHT' RESPONSE

Eyes and ears sense a threat

↓

This information is passed to the brain

↓

The brain goes on red alert and tells the adrenal glands
(on the top of the kidneys) to release extra adrenalin into
our blood vessels

↓

Blood vessels carry the adrenalin around the body

BODILY SYMPTOMS OF ANXIETY

The adrenalin carried around the body is responsible for wide-ranging physiological changes that can cause great embarrassment and fear in the anxiety sufferer as it appears that the body is totally out of control. These include:

- headaches, dizziness
- pupils dilate, blurred vision
- mouth goes dry, difficulty swallowing
- neck and shoulder muscles tense, aching neck and backache
- breathing becomes faster and shallower, supplying more oxygen to muscles (over-breathing, chest pain, tingling, palpitations, asthma)
- heart beats more rapidly as it pumps harder to send oxygen and energy to muscles in preparation for flight
- blood pressure goes up
- the sympathetic nervous system diverts blood from the skin, stomach and intestines (hence pale skin) to the heart, central nervous system, and muscles because the body is preparing for action
- stomach and guts shut down, the stomach feels knotted or has 'butterflies' which may result in indigestion, loss of appetite, nausea and stomach upsets
- liver releases stored sugar to provide fuel for quick energy (excess energy in blood)
- skin sweats to cool hot working muscles – sweating, blushing
- muscles in use are tense and ready to react faster – tension, aches and pains in muscles – 'the shakes'
- sphincter relaxes, frequent urination, diarrhoea.

To many people cats are charming animals, but Sarah cannot stand them ever since she was badly clawed as a child by a neighbour's vicious tom. If she sees one, she is immediately overcome by a feeling of strong panic and will run as fast as she can in the opposite direction. The problem is that cats are actually quite common, and many family outings have been spoiled by Sarah's fear as, after a sighting, she is a physical wreck, shaking and exhausted, and needs to go to bed for several hours to get over the shock.

THE 'FIGHT OR FLIGHT' RESPONSE TO A THREAT

It can be enormously reassuring for anxiety sufferers to realise that their frightening symptoms are actually a normal response to a threat caused by the release of adrenalin into the body. Once they understand what is going on they can normalise this process, and this in itself can lessen their anxiety.

The purpose of the physical reactions caused by the adrenalin is to increase our readiness for action by stimulating the 'fight or flight' hormone – the ideal state for someone who needs to react with a burst of energy.

For example, if you see a potentially violent person approach a little child in a car park, what do you do? Without even thinking about it, adrenalin is released, you snatch the child away from danger and run to safety with the child in your arms.

However, once you have removed yourself from the impending threat, the burst of energy deserts you, and you become a nervous wreck. Your knees are knocking, your heart is pounding, and you feel like a quivering jelly because the adrenalin was only released in response to the very objective threat of someone's life in danger.

This normal response becomes a problem when the adrenalin is not only released in response to objective threats, but becomes stimulated by subjective threats which aren't really there but are actually irrational dangers in our mind. What can then happen is that the adrenalin button can be switched on and off so much that it becomes hypersensitive and can give us panic attacks any time, anywhere. This oversensitivity can also happen when we experience too many situations that cause us stress and anxiety.

ACTIVITY
When you are anxious what physical symptoms do you experience?

_____

_____

ANXIETY AND IRRATIONAL THOUGHTS
PSYCHOLOGICAL CHANGES

Anxiety is often maintained by how we perceive situations and what we say about them to ourselves. A familiar story from the Bible contrasts two different perceptions of the same event; one perception which could be termed irrational, the other rational.

TWO DIFFERENT PERCEPTIONS (Num. 13:17-33)

The Lord told Moses to send out spies to explore the land of Canaan. 'See what the land is like and whether the people who live there are strong or weak' (v.18). After forty days, the men returned and agreed that the land was rich and fertile. However, it was populated by warlike peoples living in walled cities, and the spies disagreed about what this meant for Israel.

Caleb's positive evaluation, 'We should go up and take possession of the land, for we can certainly do it' (v.30) was in stark contrast to the majority of the spies whose fear gave them a totally different perception: 'We can't attack those people; they are stronger than we are' (v.31). 'We seemed like grasshoppers in our own eyes, and we looked the same to them' (v.33b).

This story demonstrates that how we interpret life's challenges can not only affect us emotionally with fear and anxiety, but also affect God's work. The problem seldom lies in how we gather the facts: it is our interpretation of them. Anxiety creeps in when we forget the most important fact of all – God is in control and He will lead us forward.

PSYCHOLOGICALLY BIASED THINKING

Irrational thoughts are a distorted response to the information we receive so that our opinions and perceptions are affected by a misinterpreted evaluation – the way we see a situation (which is not how it actually is) will then cause anxiety.

When we have these irrational thoughts the anxiety will be maintained, and may take the form of what is called 'catastrophic thinking'. Thinking in catastrophic ways, both by misinterpreting bodily symptoms and anticipating disaster, plays a major role in the onset of anxiety symptoms, and in making them worse. 'Anxiety thoughts' of this type include:

1. Thoughts of anticipation
Anxiety always relates to a threat, and anticipatory thoughts will

leap ahead to what might happen so that the anxious person keeps replaying everything that could possibly go wrong until they get bogged down with fear: 'I can't cope. What if this happens? What if that happens?'

Social anxiety is also often fuelled by fearful anticipatory thoughts: 'There will be nobody at the party to talk to me so I'm not going to go', or 'I might faint in the shop if I have a panic attack'. Anticipatory thoughts are very powerful and create a level of anxiety that seriously limits the quality of life of the sufferer. For example: those who fear lifts will already be asking themselves 'What if I get stuck?' while people with social anxiety will already be worrying that 'There will be nobody at the barbecue that I know'.

2. Can't cope thoughts

The second type is 'Can't cope' thoughts. These are typically expressed through negative statements such as 'I can't bear this, this is so awful' and 'I can't do that' and are related to both the situation and the symptoms. Such thoughts quickly make any existing anxiety even worse, drain our confidence levels, and encourage us to give up before we have really tried.

3. Thoughts misinterpreting bodily symptoms

A third thought type is the misinterpretation of bodily symptoms so that instead of realising that our physical bodily sensations when anxious are an automatic response caused by rising levels of adrenalin, we get increasingly worried and think there is something seriously wrong with us: 'I'm going mad', 'I am out of control', 'I'm having a heart attack', 'I'm going to pass out'. It is only when we understand our bodily symptoms that we can normalise what is happening to us.

4. Escape thoughts

The final thought pattern commonly found in catastrophic thinking is 'escape thoughts'. If you are sitting in a cinema wedged in the middle of the row, and you suddenly start thinking 'Oh, I've got a panic attack!' your natural response is to escape from the situation: 'I will be OK if I get out of here.'

However, although anxiety will appear to decrease in the short term when you leave the cinema, the long-term damaging effect is that the whole anxiety pattern has been strengthened. As a result, next time the short-term fix of the seemingly successful avoidance strategies will be adopted even more quickly. *But avoidance will maintain anxiety.*

To help anybody with these sorts of anxiety problems we must identify what their thinking pattern is, and show them that far from freeing them from anxiety they are actually making the problem worse through maintaining and feeding the catastrophic thought patterns.

Michael grew up in a family where his father worked nights and, consequently, as children they were not allowed to have friends around very often in case they disturbed his father's sleep. Michael grew up feeling ill at ease with people, but although he could cope with small numbers he increasingly found larger numbers difficult. The first time he really panicked was when he was at a cinema with his girlfriend and he suddenly felt very anxious. He was sweating, his hands were shaking, and he had an overwhelming fear that he was going to faint. 'I just couldn't stay there any longer – I had to get out.' Michael left the film halfway through, and since then being anywhere with large numbers of people has become a real problem for him. He cannot travel on a bus or train, or attend any event where there are many people. He cannot shop in a busy store or high street, and has to force himself to go to his daughter's Parents' Evening at the primary school.

ACTIVITY

Write down the sort of thoughts you have when you feel anxious:

_____

_____

ANXIETY AND OUR BEHAVIOUR
BEHAVIOURAL MAINTAINING CYCLES

The Anxiety Curve diagram opposite helps us to see what actually happens in our behaviour in relation to anxiety. If you were to ask: 'What would happen if you were to remain in the situation you fear? Would your anxiety stay the same, increase or decrease?' most anxious people would answer 'increase'. They fear that, if their anxiety continues rising, something terrible will happen such as they will faint, vomit, have a heart attack, or go mad. On the graph they imagine the line rising sharply until it goes off the page and they 'explode'.

However, this belief is not true. Experience and experiments with anxious people show that after a certain time the anxiety begins to decrease of its own accord. Therefore the more an anxious person faces the fear, the more the initial anxiety decreases and so does the time the anxiety lasts for. The graph below shows how an anxious person's anxiety will diminish as they expose themselves to face small targets. Exposure to anxiety-provoking situations using anxiety management skills is an important way forward in overcoming anxiety.

ANXIETY CURVE AND AVOIDANCE DIAGRAM

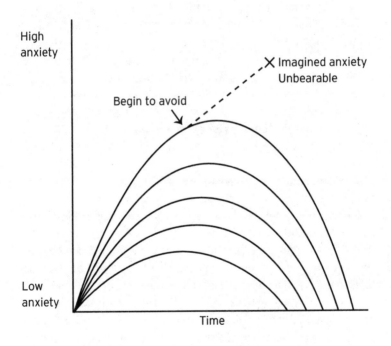

1. Avoidance and escape

One of the natural reactions to perceived danger is to *flee from it*, or *avoid it*. This is the 'fight or flight response'. However, *avoidance of*, and *escape from* simply maintain anxiety because they prevent a person from learning how to manage the anxiety.

Susy was too anxious to go shopping and had resorted to online shopping because in the past she had experienced several panic attacks inside shops. She feared that if she went into a shop her anxiety would become so intense that she would have a heart attack. Through counselling, Susy learned to press on through the anxiety with the help of learned coping strategies so that her anxiety eventually lessened, and she was able to finally conquer her fear and go shopping – treating herself to a new dress!

2. Seeking reassurance (positive reinforcer)

'Reassurance seeking' can also subtly fuel anxiety. The person who constantly seeks reassurance to boost their confidence will frequently ask, 'Am I doing OK?' However, this actually indicates that the person subconsciously has doubts that they or the situation will be OK and, because of this, it will not be long before they feel the need to seek reassurance again.

Although wanting to be reassured is a very natural tendency, it does not actually help anxiety. Chris once worked with a dentist who wanted to help some patients get over needle phobia. Before seeking her help, the dentist had been giving them tranquillisers, not realising that this was actually a positive reinforcement because the needle phobics never had to face their anxiety. Again, the patients could only find release from their heightened anxiety levels by facing their needle phobia and working through it.

While recognising that reassurance alone will never solve the root problem and that anxiety sufferers must face their fear to move on, it is not a good idea to totally abandon the anxiety sufferer in their anxious situation with the attitude that they sink or swim – a process called 'flooding'. Chris prefers a gentler approach where people are gradually exposed to their anxiety, getting them to move on step by step rather than expecting them to progress in one gigantic leap.

3. Social maintaining cycles
One example of the social maintaining cycle which nurtures a subtle (and well-meaning) maintenance of the anxiety problem is the kindly friend who does an agoraphobic person's shopping, thus allowing the sufferer to remain at home and avoid facing their fear. Such 'helpful' behaviour, although from generous motives, actually contributes to maintaining the anxiety, and fails to help the sufferer move on.

Margaret was a great believer in 'loving your neighbour' and was known for her good deeds in her church and neighbourhood. When she heard that Ros had agoraphobia, Margaret quickly became indispensable – dropping everything to be with Ros if she needed to go out anywhere. Margaret was very upset when she was told that her actions were more harmful than helpful, but she followed the advice she was given, and when Ros rang told her firmly that she could not accompany her.

'It really upset me,' said Margaret. 'Ros thought I didn't want to be her friend any more, and sometimes she would be crying and pleading for me to help her. It was so hard to turn that plea for help down.' However, as Ros gradually overcame her phobia she realised that Margaret had actually behaved like a true friend, and one of her first trips on her own was to have coffee at Margaret's house.

ACTIVITY

Can you identify your avoidance and escape behaviour when anxious?

_____

_____

REFLECTION

Read Mark 4:35–41. Imagine the scene – picture the storm, the howling gale and the fishing boat tossing on the huge waves with water crashing over the deck and soaking the disciples. They are terrified at the force of the storm and fear for their lives.

- Where is Jesus in their fear?
- Does He abandon them to their fear?
- What happens to the storm when the disciples cry out to Him for help?
- Why were they so afraid though Jesus was with them?

Now picture the anxiety that is causing you distress as the storm and visualise yourself in the boat that is in the midst of the turmoil.

- How intense is the anxiety storm? How high are its waves? What is happening to your boat?
- Where is Jesus?
- What does He say to the anxiety storm?
- What is the atmosphere in the boat if Jesus is there? What happens to the waves and wind?
- Why are you so afraid? Can you sense His peace?

PRAYER
Dear God,

Thank You that even when my mind and body make me feel as though I am in the midst of a raging storm and I am terrified that the waves of anxiety will overwhelm me, I am not on my own. Even though sometimes the sound of the raging waves and howling wind distracts me from the sense of Your presence, I know that You are there with me. I pray that just as You calmed the winds and waves when the disciples were shaking with fear, You will bring me also into calm waters. Strengthen my faith, I pray, and help me to believe that when You said, 'Quiet! Be still!' I can experience that deep peace within my own life.

Amen.

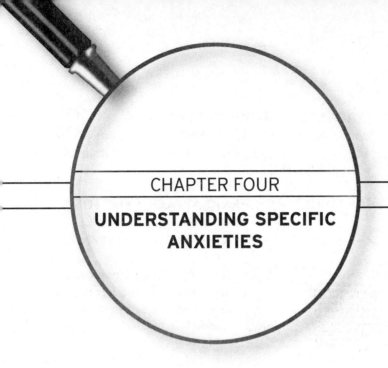

CHAPTER FOUR

UNDERSTANDING SPECIFIC ANXIETIES

INTRODUCTION

> Worry doesn't empty tomorrow of its sorrow, it empties today of its
> strength.
>
> Anon

Worry appears to be insubstantial when we try to pin it down,
but it can have devastating effects upon the sufferer and those
close to them, preventing people from living their lives to the
full, and making them slaves to their anxiety. In this chapter we
will be looking at specific anxieties in more detail, such as panic
attacks, post-traumatic stress disorder, obsessive-compulsive
disorder and GAD (generalised anxiety disorder), and the effect
they have on our lives.

AWARENESS OF ANXIETY LEVELS

Becoming aware of the level of anxiety helps educate people in the importance of keeping their anxiety below a certain level to prevent panic attacks.

A CONTINUUM FOR PANIC ATTACK SYMPTOMS

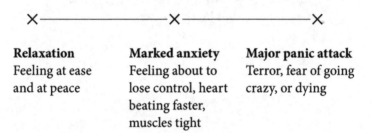

Relaxation
Feeling at ease and at peace

Marked anxiety
Feeling about to lose control, heart beating faster, muscles tight

Major panic attack
Terror, fear of going crazy, or dying

The first signs of anxiety can be quite small, and may be experienced as fleeting twinges of concern, gradually increasing in strength. Butterflies in the stomach and palpitations may follow and, as the heart beats stronger and faster and palms begin to sweat, there is often a real fear of being out of control.

At this stage the rising anxiety can be called 'marked anxiety' because it is here that anxiety becomes more of a problem. The frightened sufferer senses that they are losing control – they fear fainting (ie a perceived loss of control) and because they seem to have no power over what their body is doing they are terrified of having a panic attack which may then actually occur.

However, by understanding where their symptoms are on a continuum, people can more easily identify the level of anxiety they have reached, understand what is happening to them, and are then far more likely to be able to use strategies to stop panic attacks before the anxiety reaches that level.

CRITERIA FOR PANIC ATTACK

To ascertain whether a person is actually suffering a panic attack it can be useful to use the continuum opposite and think 'Where is this person on the continuum?'

However, one of the most useful assessments is the diagnostic health tool[1] below. The true panic attack is characterised by a period of intense anxiety, fear or discomfort in which four (or more) of the symptoms described below develop abruptly and reach a peak within ten minutes.

1. Chest pain or discomfort
2. Sensations of shortness of breath or smothering
3. Palpitations, pounding heart, or accelerated heart rate
4. Sweating
5. Chills or hot flushes
6. Feeling of choking
7. Nausea or abdominal distress
8. Trembling or shaking
9. Numbness or tingling sensation
10. Feeling dizzy, unsteady, light-headed, or faint
11. Feelings of unreality or being detached from oneself
12. Fear of losing control or going crazy
13. Fear of dying

THE PANIC ATTACK EXPERIENCE

Never underestimate how terrifying it is to experience a panic attack, an experience not helped by well-meaning friends saying things like 'Oh, don't be so silly' or 'Get a grip'. Although panic attacks generally last only a few minutes, their severity makes it seem an eternity to the sufferer, especially as some unfortunate people may have a succession of panic attacks one after the other.

Panic attacks can also make people feel very ashamed, so it's important to normalise the whole experience, and help them understand what's actually going on in their body. It can be tremendously releasing to discover that the panic attack is simply a normal physiological reaction to anxiety that has got out of control.

A common pattern is that sufferers may have been going through a very stressful time in their life, but when eighteen months later they suddenly start having panic attacks they fail to connect the two things. What seems to happen is that the body has been overstressed by coping with too much so that the adrenalin button becomes overly sensitive. Normalising what is happening is a major step in helping people to start switching off this 'fight or flight' switch.

The beliefs and fears that fuel most panic attacks include:

1. I am going to die from a heart attack.
2. I am going to die from suffocation.
3. I am going to have a stroke.
4. I am going to faint and make a fool of myself.
5. I am going crazy and having a nervous breakdown.
6. I am losing control.
7. I feel so weak I cannot move, and I am frightened of falling.
8. I am embarrassed by this, I feel ashamed of myself.

These feelings are very real to people, especially the fear of dying, but such beliefs and fears simply feed the anxiety and make it even worse. Thus, it is often beneficial to help the anxious person identify the beliefs and fears underlying their panic attacks, and challenge the distortions contained in them.

THE CYCLE OF PANIC

In panic attacks there can be a cycle of panic within the person's life. Firstly, the person experiences some sort of trigger, eg someone feels worried about the previous day's work and fears the boss's anger, making them anxious about going to work. They then get a physical reaction at work such as chest pains, breathlessness or dizziness.

The next stage is increasing distress because of the physical symptoms they are experiencing with accompanying panicky thoughts, 'I must be going mad' or 'I'm going to have a heart attack' or 'I will collapse. I can't cope.' However, when they start thinking like this, it only increases the stress and their anxiety. Finally the panic button goes and they go into a full-blown panic attack, making them say to themselves, 'I fear the fear because my body is getting out of control.'

This increases the physical reaction even more, and the whole process often repeats in a vicious circle of fear that becomes very hard for the sufferer to break, even though they find it so incapacitating.

Malcolm will never forget the first time he had a panic attack. He was a high-powered businessman and had been working long hours on a stressful project that would result in further promotion if successful. However, Malcolm was so anxious about achieving the deadline that he was having difficulty sleeping, wasn't eating properly, and survived by drinking copious amounts of black coffee. As the deadline got nearer, his stress levels got higher and higher, and suddenly he had such severe pains in his chest that he could hardly breathe. 'My vision was blurred, I was sweating heavily, and I couldn't hear because my ears were ringing. I thought I was dying.' The doctor reassured Malcolm that it was stress and not a heart attack, but a few days later he had another attack, and since then they have happened on a fairly regular basis. Paralysed by fear at the thought of experiencing further panic attacks at work, Malcolm has had to leave his high-flying job and feels depressed and isolated.

THE CYCLE OF PANIC

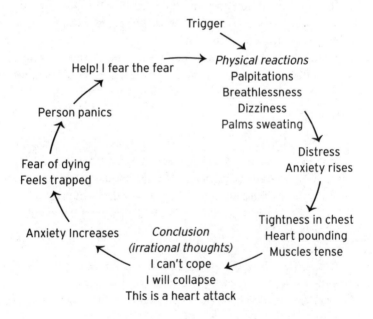

Trigger

Help! I fear the fear

Person panics

Fear of dying
Feels trapped

Anxiety Increases

Physical reactions
Palpitations
Breathlessness
Dizziness
Palms sweating

Distress
Anxiety rises

Tightness in chest
Heart pounding
Muscles tense

*Conclusion
(irrational thoughts)*
I can't cope
I will collapse
This is a heart attack

WAYS TO *MANAGE* PANIC ATTACKS

The best way to treat panic attacks, which may or may not involve hyperventilating (see below) is to understand what is happening and then face the fear with slow exposure. Forewarned is definitely forearmed in the case of the panic attack.

1. Give understanding of physiology.
2. Identify the triggers (if any).
3. Teach breathing exercise (page 88).
4. Teach relaxation exercise (page 89 or Appendix 2).
5. Identify destructive thoughts and beliefs (page 92).
6. Teach use of thought records (page 94).
7. Teach distraction (page 100).
8. Plan step by step exposure to trigger (collaboratively).

HYPERVENTILATION

About 70 per cent of panic attacks are accompanied by acute hyperventilation, although it can also be a common reaction when we experience other strong emotions such as fear, excitement, and anger.

Hyperventilation simply means over-breathing, ie breathing in excess of your body's needs. This is a relatively common problem so it is useful to know how to help people when they hyperventilate.

PHYSIOLOGY OF NORMAL BREATHING

Firstly we need to know what happens during the process of normal breathing.

1. When you breathe you take in oxygen.
2. Haemoglobin in the blood carries the oxygen to the tissues.
3. Body cells use the oxygen.
4. Carbon dioxide is released as a by-product.
5. Carbon dioxide is then carried back to lungs where it is breathed out.

PHYSIOLOGY OF HYPERVENTILATION

When adrenalin surges through your body in response to a perceived threat, muscles are tightened and it becomes more difficult to breathe properly. At this point over-breathing will occur because the body's natural response to danger is to supply the muscles with more oxygen in order that the 'fight or flight' mechanism can take effect. Let's look at this process in more detail.

There is rapid, shallow breathing from the chest rather than from the diaphragm.

↓

It causes large amounts of oxygen to be taken into the lungs which means that the heart must beat even faster to cope with this influx of oxygen.

↓

Changes in the balance between oxygen and carbon dioxide occur in the lungs.

↓

Rapid breathing in pushes out the carbon dioxide which normally forms a reservoir in the lungs.

↓

Symptoms occur because there is too little carbon dioxide in the lungs, and the blood becomes more alkaline.

↓

This in turn leads to vascular constriction resulting in diminished blood flow to the brain and other parts of the body.

↓

Eventually, if rapid breathing continues, the body may cut off this excessive supply of oxygen by causing us to faint.

↓

When we faint we return to normal patterns of breathing so fainting is a 'fail-safe' way of controlling hyperventilation.

SYMPTOMS OF HYPERVENTILATION

The symptoms caused by hyperventilation can be distressing. Because we are breathing so rapidly it makes it hard to get our breath, and so we may attempt to compensate by over-breathing because we think that will alleviate tightness in the chest.

It's important to remember that it is because there is too little carbon dioxide in our lungs and blood that symptoms such as light-headedness, feelings of faintness, a feeling of unreality, and a tingling in the limbs occur, or that sometimes our muscles become rigid and go into spasm.

Other symptoms include:

- sudden emotional outburst
- feeling too hot or too cold
- weakness
- numbness
- fatigue

- chest pain
- sweating
- clammy hands
- tremors
- swallowing difficulties.

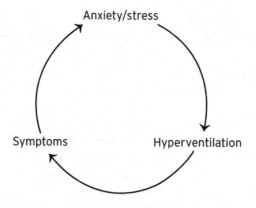

WAYS TO STOP HYPERVENTILATION

Fortunately, although hyperventilation produces frightening symptoms there are specific techniques that can bring welcome relief to the sufferer. Two things must happen in order to stop hyperventilation. Firstly, we need to help the sufferer stop over-breathing, and secondly, we need to get enough carbon dioxide back into their lungs to restore the correct balance.

When someone is hyperventilating, first get them to stop whatever they are doing. Keep calm (fear is infectious), and speak slowly, firmly and quietly. Ask them to hold their breath for as long as they comfortably can, about ten to fifteen seconds, as this will prevent the dissipation of carbon dioxide. If they can manage to do this, repeat several times, but be aware that their state of anxiety may already be too high.

One of the best ways to help hyperventilation is to improvise some sort of mask, either by using a paper bag (not plastic!) or by teaching the anxious person to cup their hands together and make a seal over their nose and mouth. Then encourage the person to breathe in through the nose (if possible) and breathe out hard through the mouth. This allows the carbon dioxide that they exhale to be breathed back into their system, correcting the balance. The person should continue to breathe in and out slowly and naturally, repeating the process four to five times (no more), by which time they should be feeling a bit better.

As the person begins to feel more in control, encourage them as they breathe to make the out-breaths longer than the in-breaths. This helps to activate the relaxation response (parasympathetic nervous system) and causes the arousal response (sympathetic nervous system) to lessen. If someone is hyperventilating, begin at a rate that feels comfortable to them, perhaps starting at breathing in for the count of three and out for six, then increasing to five/eight. For those who suffer from panic attacks it is also a good idea to practise this breathing technique for around ten minutes twice daily.

Another helpful way to stop hyperventilation is vigorous exercise – while breathing in and out through the nose, run, briskly walk, or run up and down stairs. A simple adjustment of the person's posture (if sitting or standing) so that elbows are on a level with or above the shoulders will also make it difficult to over-breathe.

Don't get upset if the person having the attack gets emotional, a common by-product of the high anxiety responsible for the panic attack. Try not to get involved in an argument or disagreement, and don't tell them off, but keep reassuring them with phrases like 'Relax … it's going to be all right', while physical touch (eg stroking the upper shoulder) may also have a calming effect. After the attack has finished, treat in the same way as shock with rest and a sweet drink, and if you still feel worried, call their doctor.

SPECIFIC TYPES OF ANXIETY
GENERALISED ANXIETY DISORDER (GAD)
This is an anxious state which is sometimes called free-floating anxiety, because it is not linked to specific situations and may be experienced on an almost daily basis. It can be triggered by various stresses at home or work, even if they are relatively minor, and is often confusing for sufferers because they themselves may have no idea why they feel so anxious. Another hallmark of people with GAD is that they are seldom anxious about just one particular thing (that is more likely to be a phobia), but the anxiety is generalised, causing a feeling of restlessness, irritability, difficulty in concentrating and poor sleep patterns.

GAD develops in about one in fifty people at some stage in life, and is diagnosed through typical symptoms that persist for at least six months. Symptoms vary from a mild feeling of anxiety to acute fear similar to that experienced by a phobia sufferer. It is common for GAD sufferers to suspect that they are going insane but, like all anxiety disorders, the condition is not connected to insanity. Relaxation exercises can help enormously, but if the anxiety experienced is very severe it may be necessary to use other strategies such as those helpful in dealing with panic attacks.

PHOBIAS

Phobias represent one of the most extreme forms of anxiety. The dictionary definition of the word phobia is 'An abnormal or morbid fear or aversion'.[2] A phobia is a persistent, abnormal, and irrational fear of a specific thing or situation that compels the sufferer to avoid it at all costs, even when given the awareness and reassurance that it is not dangerous. You can become phobic about absolutely anything, and phobia sufferers will go to extreme lengths to avoid situations or objects that they fear.

Phobias are extremely distressing. Once a phobia has got established in the mind of a person, the best way to overcome it is to persevere in slowly facing up to the crippling fear that the person experiences. A step by step planned exposure to the phobia is the usual form of treatment, and has an excellent success rate if the patient is able to complete the process. There are many different sorts of phobia including:

Agoraphobia

Agoraphobia is an abnormal fear of open spaces or public places. The agoraphobic fears being in any situation or place where they do not feel safe or where they feel trapped. This fear urges them to escape to a place of safety which is normally their own home.

The fear usually reflects an expectation that something terrible will happen to them as an individual, to loved ones, or to property. Some sufferers find that they can venture further away from their place of safety if accompanied by a trusted friend or relative. However, the agoraphobic may then become so totally reliant upon their 'carer' that they can no longer go out without help.

The agoraphobic's fear may sometimes be so overwhelming that it triggers a panic attack. This experience with its awful physiological sensations in addition to the original fear may then make it almost impossible for the sufferer to leave the safety of their home. Although understandable, this course of action actually reinforces the fear and makes recovery much harder. It is important that a sufferer realises that their brain has become conditioned, and that what has been learned can also be unlearned. Generally the only way forward is some form of exposure programme which will help them to face the fear.

Joan, forty-five, has been happily married for twenty-five years and has two teenage children. Since she experienced a panic attack whilst shopping in town – an experience she described as 'being totally reduced to a quivering jelly of fear' – she has been unable to leave the house unless someone is with her. Even a trip to the corner shop five minutes away has become impossible, and she no longer visits friends for coffee, becoming more and more isolated within her own four walls. Although Joan feels very guilty about the stress her condition is causing her family, she is unable to visualise a day when she will ever be able to go out on her own again.

Social Phobia

Social phobia is characterised by a person's fear of saying or doing something humiliating or embarrassing that will make them the focus of attention and cause others to judge them in a negative light. It is extremely inhibiting, and makes the person hypersensitive to their own behaviour as they continually worry what others are thinking about them. Actually sufferers rarely behave in a humiliating or embarrassing way, but they will 'avoid' social contact just in case they do.

It is thought that about 20 per cent of introverts suffer with social phobia. Their natural temperament and personality often result in a slow attainment of social confidence, and therefore some sufferers find it beneficial to undergo training in social skills, working on their perception of social situations and what their role is.

For teenagers under eighteen years, it is important that symptoms last for at least six months before a diagnosis of social phobia is made as many teenagers are naturally self-conscious in public. Social phobia may include behaviours such as:

- fear of public speaking
- fear of eating in public
- fear of urinating in public
- fear of blushing.

Louise, aged twenty-three, has developed social phobia and still lives at home with her parents. As a child she moved frequently because her father was in the army and this hindered her development of social skills, especially as she was often bullied at school because her accent was different and she was quite plump. As a result, Louise began to stutter at school and her mind would go blank if the teacher asked her a question. Louise began to get more and more anxious about seeming stupid.

The problem has not improved as she's got older. Louise is afraid to talk to people in case they find her boring or stupid, and if she goes out to a social occasion she will worry about it for hours beforehand, and then for hours afterwards analyse every minute detail of her behaviour. She feels so tense that nowadays she almost never goes out at all, and avoids people contact whenever she can. Consequently her workmates think that she is rude and stuck up.

Other Specific Phobias

There are clear criteria that are helpful in deciding whether a person is suffering from a phobia. The phobia sufferer will characteristically show marked and persistent fear that is unreasonable or excessive, triggered by the anticipation or presence of a specific situation or object. If the sufferer is then exposed to the feared situation or object it almost invariably provokes a strong and immediate anxiety response, and possibly a panic attack. In children, this anxiety may be expressed through crying, tantrums or clinging when faced with a feared situation or object. Phobia sufferers will do everything possible to avoid the phobic situation or, if there is no other option, exhibit intense anxiety and distress in the presence of their fear.

Specific phobias include:
- animals
- natural environment – heights, storms, water
- blood – injections
- situational – flying, lifts, enclosed spaces (eg cinema)
- situations that may lead to choking, vomiting or contact with an illness
- in children, loud sounds, costumed characters.

POST-TRAUMATIC STRESS DISORDER (PTSD)

The World Health Organization defines PTSD as 'a delayed or protracted response to a stressful event or situation (either short- or long-lasting) of an exceptionally threatening or long-lasting nature which is likely to cause pervasive distress in almost anyone'.

PTSD occurs when a person has been exposed to a traumatic event where they experienced or witnessed an event(s) that involved actual or threatened death, serious injury, or was a physical threat to self or others, giving rise to a response that involved intense fear, helplessness, or horror.

For the person caught up in one of these catastrophic traumatic events, there is a high possibility that PTSD will be an outcome, with one in four being affected. PTSD is more likely if the person can see no way of escaping the situation, and is also increased by the previous number of traumas a person has gone through (accumulative).

Other factors are the existence of current stressors within the person's life, and a pre-sensitivity such as that demonstrated by artistic and sensitive people with vivid imaginations. For the latter group, giving them a critical debriefing and encouraging them to talk about it too quickly is counterproductive as it will traumatise them further and get programmed into their imagination.

In the aftermath of such an experience, many people feel shocked, numb, dazed and disorientated, and do not want to talk about what has happened. In the first instance, survivors have said that what they found most helpful was practical advice, information, and support with day-to-day tasks.

The Symptoms of PTSD

PTSD is present when the traumatic event is persistently re-experienced with distressing recurrent and intrusive recollections of the event, including images, thoughts or perceptions, nightmares, and/or flashback. Intense psychological distress will also flare up with any exposure to internal or external triggers that symbolise or resemble an aspect of the traumatic event.

PTSD is also characterised by the sufferer's persistent avoidance of stimuli associated with trauma in three or more of the following:

- Efforts to avoid thoughts, feelings, or conversations associated with the trauma.
- Efforts to avoid activities, places, or people that arouse recollections of the trauma.
- Inability to recall an important aspect of the trauma.
- Feeling of detachment from others.
- Marked diminished interest and/or participation in significant activities.
- Restricted range of feelings (unable to have loving feelings).
- Sense of future being foreshortened.

Persistent symptoms of increased arousal (not present before trauma) are also an indication that PTSD is present, although these symptoms must occur consistently for at least a month after the event before a diagnosis is given. PTSD is indicated when two or more of the following are present:

- difficulty falling or staying asleep
- irritability or outbursts of anger

- difficulty in concentrating
- hyper-vigilance
- exaggerated startle response.

A full diagnosis for PTSD can be found in the *Diagnostic and Statistical Manual for Mental Disorders*.[3]

Managing PTSD

For PTSD sufferers, expressing their feelings relating to the trauma by talking about it may be the best way of coming to terms with their experience. However, professional views differ on whether or not counselling or some form of psychological debriefing immediately after the event can prevent serious problems developing later. A number of studies have indicated that quick drug intervention and too hasty counselling into post-traumatic stress is counterproductive, and is not just unhelpful but actually harmful. The National Institute for Clinical Excellence (NICE) supports this view.

Everyone affected by PTSD has their own unique response, and needs to proceed at their own pace. What's important is that there is an opportunity to talk to someone about their distress when they're ready to do so.

Treatments for PTSD are still being evaluated, but experts agree that for anyone who is still suffering months after the event, the most effective approach is a series of in-depth sessions with a psychologist or other therapist. During these sessions, the sufferer will be encouraged to go over the experience in detail.

Vera, sixty-eight, was involved in a car accident which was followed by a long stay in hospital while she recovered from a broken pelvis. Since then she will not go anywhere by car, and still sleeps badly because of recurrent nightmares about the crash: 'I see the other driver speeding towards us and have the terrible sense that he will hit us head on, but am powerless to stop it.' Even in the daytime she has vivid flashbacks of the scene, and because cars cause her such distress Vera has stopped watching television because of car adverts and storylines involving crashes.

OBSESSIVE-COMPULSIVE DISORDER (OCD)

People with obsessive-compulsive disorder suffer intensely from recurrent and persistent thoughts, and impulses or images (obsessions) such as fear of contamination, although the person recognises these thoughts as irrational and the product of their own mind.

Examples of obsessions are:	Examples of compulsions are:
fear of shameful behaviour	cleaning
contamination	checking
perverted sexual thoughts	washing
symmetrical arrangements	measuring
intrusive thoughts and images	repeating actions or tasks
unsatisfactory body images	confessing imaginary 'sins'

The compulsions triggered by the obsessive thoughts take the form of repetitive behaviours which the sufferer performs to alleviate their distress. However, these physical rituals such as excessive washing, cleaning, checking, or confessing imaginary 'sins' only bring temporary relief because the ritual must be repeated or the person's anxiety significantly increases. To be diagnosed as OCD the rituals must take up more than one hour a day, or significantly interfere with the person's normal daily routine.

OCD can be overcome with a type of behaviour therapy known as 'exposure and response prevention'. In this approach a person is deliberately and voluntarily exposed to whatever triggers the obsessive thoughts, and then taught techniques to deal with the anxiety and avoid performing the compulsive rituals, sometimes in conjunction with anti-depressant therapy. Recovery is usually slow, but hard work produces positive rewards and complete recovery can be achieved.

Every time Geoff left the house he had to check at least ten times that he had locked the front door, which frequently made him late for work. By learning breathing skills to help reduce the physiological symptoms of anxiety, and finding ways to distract his thoughts away from the obsessive images that accompanied this ritual, Geoff began to work on checking the door one less time every week. Over about twelve weeks he was able to reduce the number of times he compulsively checked the front door, and can now walk away without checking. Although he still feels some anxiety, he is able to manage it, rather than let the anxiety dictate his behaviour.

ACTIVITY

Have you struggled with any of these specific anxieties? If so, from what you have learned so far, how can you help yourself?

_____

_____

REFLECTION

Look at the following two passages:

Isaiah 43:1–2

- What does God say of Israel? (v.1). Read the verse out loud and replace the names of Jacob and Israel with your own. Why does God tell us not to fear?
- What sort of situations does God tell us He will be with us in? Do you think these are situations that would cause anxiety? Picture God with you in your situation, picture Him being with you in the waters, through the rivers, in the fire, through the flames – carrying you.

Matthew 6:25–34

- Go for a walk or sit in your garden and look around you at trees, flowers, animals, birds etc, or watch a natural history programme on the television. Read this passage slowly and take inspiration from the way that God cares for His natural creation. How much are you worth to your Father? How much was He willing to pay for you? What does this passage suggest as an antidote to worry (v.33)?

PRAYER

Thank You, God, that You call me by my name and I am Yours. Thank You that You will be with me when it seems that I am walking through a fiery furnace as I struggle to deal with my emotions, and that I do not need to be afraid because You are my Redeemer. Thank You also for the beauty of Your creation that brings me peace in my darkest moments. Thank You that I am fearfully and wonderfully made, and that if I submit myself to Your loving hands, You are able to reshape me and turn me into a beautiful vessel that reflects Your glory.

Amen.

CHAPTER FIVE

SKILLS TO HELP OVERCOME ANXIETY

INTRODUCTION

Sow a thought,
Reap an act:
Sow an act,
Reap a habit:
Sow a habit,
Reap a character:
Sow a character,
Reap a destiny.
   Ralph Waldo Emerson

Skills and strategies are available to deal successfully with all sorts of anxiety disorders including generalised anxiety disorder, phobias and obsessive-compulsive disorder. As the CWR Wholeness Model shows (page 22), we are made up of different areas, and there are strategies to help us, physically, emotionally, behaviourally, mentally and spiritually. By persevering in the use of these skills the stranglehold of your anxiety will begin to loosen, although sometimes people with acute anxiety may also require medication to help them function well enough to work on using these anxiety management skills.

ANXIETY AND OUR BODIES
PHYSIOLOGICAL CHANGE

SKILLS TO REDUCE PHYSICAL SYMPTOMS OF ANXIETY

1. Breathing exercise: Breathing ourselves calm
Make sure you are sitting comfortably with your feet slightly apart, and with your eyes closed or looking down. Be aware of the chair taking your weight, and become responsive to how still you are, ignoring noises or intrusive thoughts. Try putting any distractions away in an imaginary box … just think of peace and calm.

Now become aware of your slow breathing, in and out of your nose, and continue for a few breaths. Note whether you find the in-breath (inhalation) or out-breath (exhalation) more comfortable. Continue to breathe slowly. Now count how long your in-breath is and how long your out-breath takes. Carry on breathing to identify this rhythm, and stay with it.

Continuing with your in-breath the same, make your out-breath about two counts longer (eg if your in-breath is a slow three, make your out-breath five). Stay with this, breathing gently without forcing any breaths. Every time you breathe out, do it slowly with a sigh, rather like a balloon deflating. Continue for a few more minutes to deeply breathe and relax. Note how much more relaxed the body is, and how your anxiety is reducing.

2. Relaxation

Relaxation is incompatible with feeling anxious because relaxation is controlled by the parasympathetic nervous system and not the sympathetic nervous system, which is responsible for triggering the adrenalin that provokes strong anxiety responses.

Many forms of relaxation techniques such as meditating on Scripture or using imagery help switch our minds off from anxiety, or we can relax just by doing something that we enjoy such as these options suggested by delegates at a recent conference.

A warm bath
Fly-fishing
Walking
Relaxing whilst listening to music
Playing an instrument
Reading
Writing
Gardening
Scrabble
Praying
Laughing
'Crashing out'
Glass of wine with a friend

RELAXATION EXERCISES

Relaxation is a skill, and to acquire the habit of relaxation we need to practise it regularly – perhaps initially daily for a month until the feeling of relaxation becomes familiar to us. The ideal setting for any relaxation exercise is somewhere without distractions such as sitting or lying down in a quiet room.

One excellent relaxation technique used by counsellors is known as 'progressive relaxation', first developed by an American psychologist, Jacobson, in 1938, and later refined by a general practitioner, Wolpe, and a psychologist, Lazarus, in 1966. It consists of tensing different muscle groups for about six seconds, and then relaxing them for a longer period. This very simple relaxation exercise is often called 'tensing and relaxing' and concentrates on four areas – the face and neck; shoulders and arms; chest, stomach and lower back; and hips, thighs and legs.

ACTIVITY
TENSING AND RELAXING EXERCISE

Begin as in the breathing exercise with feet slightly apart, eyes looking down or closed, as you again feel the chair take your weight, and rid yourself of intrusive thoughts. Focus on your breathing again, and try to make your out-breath two counts longer than your in-breath.

Now focus on your right hand. Squeeze it tightly into a fist, clenching it tighter and tighter, and be aware of the tension as you do so. Hold for six seconds. Then let the tension go and relax your fingers, letting them go loose for about ten seconds. Repeat.

Now flex your right elbow, tensing your arm and forcing your right knuckle into your right shoulder. Hold this tense position for six seconds, then let your arm go floppy, totally relaxed, and notice the difference. Repeat. Now repeat this with your left hand and arm, then pull your shoulders up to your ears, tense them tightly, and then relax once more.

Continue relaxing other parts of the body in the same way, working upward via your neck and facial muscles; then downwards using your stomach muscles and buttock muscles continuing through hips, thighs, legs, ankles and lastly by curling up your toes. It may be helpful to think of the words 'calm' or 'peace' each time you breathe out and relax your muscles. Having done this, if you are aware that a particular part of your body still feels tense, repeat the tensing and relaxing exercise for those muscles.

Once your body is relaxed, picture a place that feels very safe to you – a garden, a room, or a favourite part of the countryside, and then ask Jesus to walk with you there. Is He saying anything to you or are you just relaxing in His company? Soak up the peaceful atmosphere and when you are ready, open your eyes and stretch out. This exercise is now complete. You may also like to try the alternative relaxation exercise in Appendix 2.

PHYSICAL EXERCISE

Another way to deal with the physical aspect of anxiety is to combat it with vigorous physical exercise such as walking, jogging, squash, football etc. Studies show that aerobic physical exercise is not only healthy, but can also reduce muscle tension and relieve frustration.

ANXIETY AND IRRATIONAL THOUGHTS
PSYCHOLOGICAL CHANGE

SKILLS TO REDUCE WORRYING THOUGHTS
Very often it is the views and opinions we hold that cause us anxiety, and accordingly we may have to work on changing our thought life. The two main ways which have proved effective in breaking the cycle of worry are:

1. challenging and replacing irrational thoughts
2. distraction.

1. CHALLENGING UNHELPFUL AND IRRATIONAL THOUGHTS
A useful tool to help us challenge our irrational and unhelpful thoughts is the 'A-W-A-R-E' skill which helps us to look at our anxiety more objectively.

THE 'A-W-A-R-E' SKILL
Step 1: Acknowledge and accept your anxiety
The more people fight anxiety, the more difficult it is to get rid of the anxious feelings. A more constructive approach is to accept the anxiety and work with it. One way is to imagine the anxiety as a shape or even an animal, making it easier to work on the problem as the sufferer can then look at their anxiety more objectively.

Step 2: Watch your anxiety
It can be very helpful to take on the role of a curious observer, monitoring the anxiety's intensity and noting when it peaks and

subsides, rating it on a scale from one to ten. Remember you are not your anxiety. Be in the anxiety state, but not of it.

Once the anxiety has been assessed, work towards bringing the level down – a far more realistic target than expecting the anxiety to totally disappear, as setting out with a fixed, concrete goal to eradicate the anxiety will often bring even more anxiety and guilt if the goal is not reached!

Step 3: Act with your anxiety
As far as possible keep behaving normally, and aim to do what you set out to do. Breathe normally in a relaxed way, and stay with the anxiety rather than running away. This will help to de-condition the anxiety.

Step 4: Replace your irrational thoughts
Learn to *challenge* irrational thinking through asking questions such as:

- What evidence do I have to support my thoughts?
- What evidence do I have against them?
- What alternative views are there?
- What would God say about my thoughts?
- What effect does my thinking have on what I do?
- Is this helpful for my long-term goal?

Step 5: Expect to improve and overcome anxiety
Expect the anxiety to get better because it will get better. Although it may not be totally overcome, it can be lessened so that it is manageable. Recognise that what you fear may never happen, and reinforce your progress with positive statements,

eg 'Learning new skills will help me to effectively handle my anxiety, and it will get less.'

ACTIVITY

Write each irrational thought down on one side of a piece of paper, and then write a true rational thought opposite which either challenges the irrational idea or gives an alternative way of looking at the situation. For example:

Worrying thoughts and images	Alternative thoughts and views
I'll never beat this anxiety.	Just take one day at a time. There are lots of things I can do to help myself.
I may have a panic attack and faint.	I've never fainted before. If I control my breathing I will be fine.
I can't face my boss – she's so critical.	Avoiding situations just makes things worse. I am going to learn to speak up for myself, and let her know how I feel. I am going to be assertive in this situation.

ACTIVITY
MAKING A THOUGHT RECORD

A thought record teaches us how to identify the link between anxiety and thoughts, and helps us learn how to test and evaluate these thoughts in order to change them. Look at the sample thought record page illustrated (on pages 96/97), and then return to the anxiety-provoking situation that you used when filling in the CWR Wholeness Model or Alternative Anxiety Model earlier. Now use this situation as a focus to record your thought responses in your own thought record (a blank thought record page can be found in Appendix 3). Note the triggering event, the intensity of your anxiety, and your irrational self-talk. Now challenge the thoughts by looking at them objectively, based on the evidence you have, and then write in a new, more balanced, rational thought. Say the new self-talk out loud to reinforce the positive thoughts and help your anxiety.

THOUGHT RECORD (Read across both pages)

Trigger	Mood	Self-talk/images
Who? What? When? Where?	Describe feeling in one word. Now rate intensity of mood (0-10).	What was going through your mind just before you started to feel this way? What images or memories come to mind?
Exams	Anxiety (10)	What if I don't pass? I shall be a failure. If I fail it will be awful because then I won't get promotion.
Friday pm Out shopping and about to go up in a lift	Panic (9) Anxiety (10)	I am having palpitations and feel faint. I am having a heart attack. I am going to embarrass myself. Image: Lying on the floor unconscious with people laughing at me.

Evidence	New self-talk	Re-rate mood
What factual evidence supports this thought? What factual evidence doesn't support this thought?	*Write an alternative and/or balanced thought.* *Write an alternative view of the situation that is consistent with the evidence.*	*Re-rate the intensity of the feeling. Hopefully it will have become lower.*
I have had 100 per cent pass rate with all my exams. God doesn't see me as a failure. It's the firm's policy that I won't get promotion if I fail.	I am very unlikely to fail. If I do, that doesn't mean I am a failure - my best is good enough - God sees me as a person of infinite worth whether I fail or not. (Isa. 43:4) If I don't get promotion, God still has a plan for my life. (Eph. 1:11-12)	Anxiety (6-7)
A rapid heartbeat doesn't mean I am having a heart attack. Feeling faint with palpitations is all part of anxiety. I have never fainted or had anything wrong with my heart. I have seen a person faint, and nobody laughed. Everyone was helpful and sympathetic.	My doctor reassured me that palpitations are not necessarily dangerous - he said they are more likely to be a symptom of anxiety. In all likelihood my heart will return to normal in a few minutes. I can use the skills I have learnt to manage my anxiety and reduce the symptoms. I have never fainted before, but if I do people are more likely to be helpful and sympathetic than laugh at me. With God's help I am learning how to overcome anxiety. (Isa. 41:10; Phil. 4:13)	Panic (5) Anxiety (5)

FINDING ALTERNATIVE WAYS OF THINKING

Although speaking the truth to ourselves is a helpful way of coping with worrying thoughts, not all anxiety sufferers find this easy. An alternative approach can be in asking questions that encourage a logical rather than an emotional response such as, 'Are there any reasons for you having worrying thoughts? What is the evidence for what you fear?'

Rachel couldn't stop worrying about the possibility of a global water drought, and was having trouble sleeping as she vividly imagined what a catastrophe this would be with the death of the elderly and little children. She was encouraged to look at the actual evidence by researching the topic on the internet. Rachel realised that although there was evidence that humankind needed to husband water more responsibly, there was no real basis for her overwhelming fears, and as she began to feed her mind with truth her worrying thoughts decreased significantly.

Another way to help people explore their anxiety is by asking the following questions: 'What is the worst thing that can happen?' 'What is the best thing that can happen?' 'What is likely to happen?' 'If the worst scenario were to happen, what measures could you put in place to cope?' Questions like these really help people face their anxiety.

Mel was living in a real anxiety state caused by worry about what she would do if her elderly mother died, although there was no actual evidence to suggest that this would happen in the immediate future. In counselling, Mel was encouraged to face the issue head on with the direct question, 'How would you cope if your mother died?'

As Mel and her counsellor explored answers to this question together, Mel considered various options: 'If she died, I could do this, or I could do that' and, as a result, her anxiety levels dramatically decreased because she now had a plan of action.

Another helpful tool that counsellors use in encouraging an objective view is to ask the sufferer what they would say to someone else in the same situation, and then suggest that they take their own advice!

ACTIVITY

Replace these worrying thoughts with new alternative balanced thoughts that challenge the anxiety expressed:

Sara is late for our meeting. Her car might have crashed and she may be injured.

_____

I am beginning to sweat and feel sick. I will have to dash to the toilet and that will embarrass me.

_____

I'm anxious that I cannot cope by myself because my husband has left me.

_____

Now make up some examples of your own:

_____

_____

_____

2. DISTRACTION

Distraction is a simple but very effective way to cope with irrational thoughts, and can even have a fun element. One option you might like is mental games – engaging your mind in activities such as mental arithmetic, reciting poetry, Scripture, crosswords or simply counting backwards from one hundred by threes, eg ninety-seven, ninety-four, ninety-one etc.

Another helpful alternative is to focus on the outside world to distract you, perhaps by listening to a conversation, looking at what colours people are wearing or listing all the things you can hear, see or touch.

We can also engage in the biblical approach to distraction by fixing our gaze upon God: 'If you value the approval of God, fix your minds on whatever is true and honourable and just and pure and lovely and admirable' (Phil. 4:8, Phillips).

When Chris's daughter was ill, anxious thoughts such as 'What if this happens?' 'What if that happens?' kept waking Chris up in the middle of the night so that she felt absolutely worn out. To cope with this anxiety Chris learned to take a favourite worship song – *All hail the Lamb, enthroned on high*[1] – and sing it inwardly whenever her thoughts were running rampage in the middle of the night. Sometimes she would have to do this a number of times before the anxiety subsided, but over time the whole thing got easier as Chris worshipped instead of worrying.

After about a year, although Chris's situation hadn't changed and her daughter was still ill, her anxiety levels had dramatically decreased as she found herself waking in the middle of the night with the words of the song already on her mind.

Mark was very anxious about travelling on trains. He could just about get to the station, but was not able to actually get on the train. It was agreed with his counsellor that, armed with his newly learned skills of breathing and distraction, he would board the train and travel just one stop up the line. When standing on the platform Mark looked across to the opposite platform and performed a number of distracting counting tasks. 'How many people are wearing red coats? How many black? How many people are wearing glasses? How many are wearing jeans?' Mark found that because his thoughts were occupied by the distraction of looking out for all these things, the feelings of anxiety did not arise. He is now able to get on the train and, having achieved success once, travels on the train without a problem.

The use of imagery techniques can be very powerful. 'You will guard him *and* keep him in perfect *and* constant peace whose mind [both its inclination and its character] is stayed on You, because he commits himself to You, leans on You *and* hopes confidently in You' (Isa. 26:3, Amplified). For instance, when an image associated with the anxiety comes up learn to replace it with an image of God as a strong tower (eg Psa. 61:3) or as the Rock on which you stand. Alternatively, imagine comforting homely images like being wrapped in a warm blanket, or try simple physical distractions such as going for a walk or behavioural activities such as seeing friends.

Meditation quietens your mind and brings a feeling of peace, while another useful tool is the 'traffic lights' distraction technique for stopping unhelpful thought processes. As soon as you start saying negative statements about yourself – 'I'm no good. I'm a failure. This is terrible' – mentally picture a red traffic light: 'Stop! Red traffic light!' and say to yourself, 'I'm not going down that road.' At this point think of new helpful thoughts and visualise the traffic light turning green, allowing you to move off down the road of your new thoughts.

John was having so many anxious thoughts relating to his work that his physical symptoms made it difficult for him to function properly. He used the 'Stop! Red traffic light' skill to very good effect as he recognised he could choose to take control over stopping his thoughts. His physiological symptoms dramatically reduced, and he was soon able to concentrate again at work and improve his performance.

You can also distract yourself from anxious thoughts by the use of a bridging object. This is an object that represents security to you, perhaps associated with happy memories, eg a favourite teddy or a family photograph. It works by helping bridge from the anxiety-provoking 'here and now' to something that felt safe in the past or a specific memory that evokes good feelings. This is particularly useful for people who have suffered abuse as it helps to provide an alternative focus for their anxious thoughts.

ANXIETY AND OUR BEHAVIOUR

CHANGING BEHAVIOURAL MAINTAINING CYCLES THROUGH SKILLS TO REDUCE UNHELPFUL BEHAVIOUR

Once we understand what is happening when we feel anxious, the next stage is to overcome patterns of avoidance. It can be helpful to draw up a list of all the things you have been avoiding, or currently find difficult to achieve.

A typical list may be:

- Avoiding public transport
- Letting people take advantage of you
- Avoiding being assertive with the boss
- Constantly saying 'No' to social invitations

BREAKING ANXIETY DOWN INTO MANAGEABLE STAGES

To change anxious behaviour patterns it is important to break the behaviour down into manageable stages, ie into small achievable goals. For example, if the problem is driving a car around town and a person's goal is to be able to park the car in order to go shopping, we can break it down into several steps as in the following 'ladder' diagram. This represents a 'hierarchy of fear' where the thought of getting to the car park provokes the highest level of anxiety.

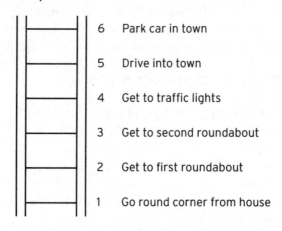

6   Park car in town

5   Drive into town

4   Get to traffic lights

3   Get to second roundabout

2   Get to first roundabout

1   Go round corner from house

Starting from the bottom the person systematically faces up to the feared situation step by step but, just like climbing a ladder, it is important to feel comfortable with each stage before progressing further. Therefore, each task is performed several times to increase confidence levels, and the sufferer may also find it helpful to score units of anxiety to help monitor their progress.

If the anxiety fails to reduce, or the person has problems facing the feared situation, the rungs on their ladder may be too far apart, and additional steps should be included to break the situation down still further.

Working with the anxiety through gradual exposure, setting small achievable goals, and giving the sufferer tools and skills (eg breathing, relaxing, distraction, helpful thoughts) helps reduce anxiety, and practising each stage until the anxiety is manageable will see real results. Using this graded behavioural technique helps overcome fears and regains lost confidence.

David had loved driving in the past, but now couldn't even be a passenger because of his severe anxiety. To help David, a laddering system was drawn up, establishing that his long-term goal at the top of the ladder was to be able to drive on the motorway again. This was then broken down into small achievable goals.

Looking at his local road map, his counsellor asked, 'What shall we try for the first target?' David replied, 'I would like to try to get to the first roundabout, but I am frightened of having a panic attack.'

His counsellor then worked with David on breathing and relaxation skills as they looked at what he could do if a panic attack made him feel unsafe driving. Their contingency plan was to pull into the side, and put hazard lights on as if the car had broken down so that nobody would know that David was feeling panicky, making him feel safer. An alternative solution was to turn into a side road, and sit for a few minutes to calm down.

The counsellor accompanied David in the car, talking calmly to him and telling him to breathe slowly. However, David felt panicky and unsafe, so they turned off into a side road, and David used his new breathing skills. Once he had calmed down the return journey went much better, and David's levels of anxiety decreased.

David practised this daily for a week until his anxiety levels were greatly reduced for this part of the journey and he had even managed to drive to the next roundabout. He was then asked, 'What is your next target?' However, David was very stressed by the next section as it had traffic lights, and he was frightened that stopping would trigger a panic attack. To combat this fear he was taught some helpful distraction techniques he could use while waiting for the lights to change, and again the counsellor went with him in the car, extending his journey this time to the traffic lights.

Although David felt very anxious, sweaty, with his hands shaking, he managed to face his fear and sit in the queue without a panic attack. Gradually, he managed to achieve each level set until finally the goal was reached, and he is now able to drive regularly on the motorway with no panic attacks.

ACTIVITY

Experiment with this behavioural activity and see if it is helpful. Make a Worry Box by finding a box or tin with a lid. Write your worries down on pieces of paper, put them into the container, and don't look at them again until the following week when you may find, like Arthur Rank below, that your worry has ceased to be a problem.

Arthur Rank, an English executive, decided to do all his worrying on one day each week. He chose Wednesdays. When anything happened that gave him anxiety and annoyed his ulcer he would write it down and put it in his worry box and forget about it until the next Wednesday. The interesting thing was that on the following Wednesday when he opened his worry box he found that most of the things that had worried him during the past six days had been settled.[2]

ANXIETY AND OUR SPIRITUAL LIFE

BECOMING MORE DEPENDENT UPON GOD

Said the robin to the sparrow:
'I should really like to know
Why these anxious human beings
Rush about and worry so.'

Said the sparrow to the robin:
'Friend, I think that it must be
That they have no heavenly Father
Such as cares for you and me.'[3]

It can be very difficult as a Christian when we suffer with intense anxiety because we constantly hear the message that Christians are *supposed* to feel full of joy and peace! However, the truth is that we are all on a journey of deepening our faith, and we all struggle in different ways.

For those who are anxious, the very last thing they need is for other Christians to heap guilt on them by saying things like, 'Well, you should trust God in that.' Of course the anxious Christian wants to trust God, but it is a battle.

Chris once came across a quote that really helped her in the times when she found it hard to keep her head above water:

'Those that struggle well are mature Christians.' Just because you struggle does not disqualify you in the Christian life – in fact, struggle is often a time of real growth for us as, when we are surrounded with anxieties, we learn to look more to God for help, recognising our weakness and becoming more dependent on Him.

LEARNING TO TRUST GOD WHEN LIFE SEEMS UNCERTAIN

> God never built a Christian strong enough to carry today's duties and tomorrow's anxieties piled on the top of them.
>
> Theodore L. Cuyler

When we are beset by anxiety God can meet us in our need, but to reach that place of trust in Him we must pass through several key stages.

A – Admit your anxiety to God
God can only help us when we admit we have a problem and need His help. Follow David's example in Psalm 142, and be totally honest about how you really feel.

B – Believe that God hears you and is in control
One of the great truths of the Bible is that God is able to guide His people in every circumstance. We read in 2 Corinthians 5:7: 'We live by faith, not by sight', and that means that we can trust God in the difficult times as well as the good times, knowing that He is in ultimate control of our life.

'What do I trust God for?' Chris asked herself that question many times when she was experiencing the pain of her daughter's illness. She obviously hoped that God would heal her daughter, but she knew that He might not do that.

So what could Chris trust God for? She trusted Him to be with her in the situation. Just like a trusting child she could put her hand in her Father's hand, knowing they were walking the path together. She trusted that He loved her, recognising how precious she was to God because He had sent Jesus to die for her, and that He was her living hope.

Feelings are deceptive and will let us down – faith is not based on feelings, but on our knowledge of God's character. God is the one certain factor in our uncertainty. For Chris, placing her trust in such a faithful God meant that she knew He would help her to cope.

C – *Consider* and *confess*

Consider what you can do about a situation – what you can change and what you can't. Confess your anxiety to God and ask for His forgiveness (see 1 John 1:9). However, be careful not to feel condemned when well-meaning Christians say things like 'But you shouldn't be anxious. God says don't be anxious about anything. Cast all your cares on Him' (see 1 Pet. 5:7) for there is 'no condemnation for those who are in Christ Jesus' (Rom. 8:1).

D – *Do*

Receive God's forgiveness, and work on replacing the lies that anxiety whispers into the mind with God's truth. Use helpful techniques like imagery, and especially words of Scripture which can become anchors to stop people slipping into despair. Be like David in the cave where, although he felt utterly distraught and poured out his anxious feelings ('I cry out to You, God. Where are You? I am pouring out my complaint to You!'), he held on to the anchoring fact, '*But* God is my refuge.' David acknowledged his feelings with total honesty, but then stopped the free fall as he confessed the truth.

When helping anxiety sufferers, keep pointing them to God's truth:

> Delight yourself in God; yes, find your joy in him at all times ... Don't worry over anything whatever; tell God every detail of your needs in earnest and thankful prayer, and the peace of God, which transcends human understanding, will keep constant guard over your hearts and minds as they rest in Christ Jesus.
>
> Phil. 4:4–7, Phillips

In these verses we find a simple formula for conquering anxiety:

Praise + Prayer = Peace.

ACTIVITY
Think of some Bible verses and Bible stories that could be used to help someone with anxiety.

_____

_____

_____

Jean could not rest because she was constantly cleaning to try and keep her house absolutely immaculate. She would work for hours scrubbing and polishing, from very early in the morning to very late at night, driven by her need to make the house absolutely spotless. Looking back to her childhood, Jean realised that she was trying to be a perfect wife because her father had left her mother, saying that she didn't know how to keep a proper home, and she felt anxious that her husband would leave her if she did not keep the house gleaming: 'I must have a perfect house.'

Once she recognised this underlying fear, she admitted her anxiety to God and asked Him to forgive her. Jean then chose to *do* something about her perfectionism, and worked towards gradually reducing the amount of housework she did each day. Finally, she was able to find time to do things that she actually enjoyed, like meeting up with friends for coffee or going swimming. Jean said that the main thing was that she realised she would never be able to achieve perfection, but that her husband and God loved her just the same.

ACTIVITY
USE OF IMAGERY

Cast all your anxiety on him because he cares for you.

1 Pet. 5:7

Sit in a place where you can be quiet and comfortable, allowing the chair to take your weight. Make sure your back is straight, your shoulders relaxed with your hands resting on your thighs, and both your feet flat on the ground. Now become aware of your natural breathing rhythm. Take deep slow breaths in and out. Try and make your out-breaths longer than your in-breaths because this relaxes your whole body more. Now become aware of a place of stillness in your mind or body – a place where you feel calm.

Once you have reached this place of stillness, visualise the issue which is causing you anxiety, and hold it in your hands. What does this anxiety feel like in your hands? Be aware of its weight – does it have a colour or a shape?

Now visualise Jesus sitting on His heavenly throne at the top of a flight of steps. Deliberately walk towards Him and climb those steep steps, carrying the anxiety in the palms of your hands.

Now place your anxiety into Jesus' hands (this is where you cast your anxiety upon Him), for He will carry the anxiety for you. Allow yourself to leave your anxiety with Jesus, and visualise turning away from Jesus, and deliberately walking away empty-handed, thus leaving your anxiety behind for Jesus to carry. You are less tempted to pick it up again if you turn your back on it!

Now be aware of how it feels to have let the anxiety go. Stay in this place of peace and calm. When you are ready, slowly open your eyes, and come back into the reality of the room. Have a stretch, and then continue with everyday life.

Jesus is now carrying your anxiety.

REFLECTION

'… I have learned to be content whatever the circumstances', wrote the apostle Paul (Phil. 4:11). That doesn't just mean when our circumstances are going well, when the sun is shining on us and we feel good about everything, but also when we find ourselves besieged by difficulties and when we are attacked by fears on all sides. Read Philippians 4, noting verses 6 and 7. Read it again slowly, out loud. Give God your anxiety, let Him take the weight from you – picture it rolling from your shoulders as you stand in God's presence like Christian's burden in *The Pilgrim's Progress*.[4] Ask for God's peace to fill you from the tips of your toes to the top of your head, the same contentment 'whatever the circumstances' that Paul had.

Drop thy still dews of quietness.
Till all our striving cease;
Take from our souls the strain and stress,
And let our ordered lives confess
The beauty of thy peace.[5]

PRAYER

I know that Your love surrounds me every single moment of every single day, Lord. Thank You so much that You understand my humanity, and the times when I become anxious. Help me to remember in those moments that You are my refuge, and my security. Since I have known You, it has changed my life for ever – I cannot live without You, nor would I want to. Help me not to keep trying to do things my own way, but to follow You with my whole heart. Thank You that life with You is an adventure. I am looking forward to all that You have in store for me, of walking beside You with my hand in Yours.
Amen.

May the God of hope fill you with all joy and peace as you trust in him ...

Rom. 15:13

APPENDIX 1

HELPING AN ANXIETY SUFFERER

When coming alongside someone with anxiety it can be helpful to make an outline of what is happening to them, and use this as a springboard to work on practical strategies to move them forward, eg 'What tools and skills may be helpful for their rational thoughts? What strategy may be helpful for their behaviour? How can they be helped to grow spiritually?'

1. What sort of anxiety is the person suffering with?

_____

_____

_____

2. How is their anxiety affecting the different areas of their lives?

Physical

_____

Thoughts

_____

Behaviour

_____

Spiritual

_____

3. Where might you start to help them?

_____

_____

_____

4. What tools and skills would you use to help each area of their lives?
(Choose one skill or tool for each area)

Physical

_____

Thoughts

_____

Behaviour

_____

Spiritual

_____

APPENDIX 2

ALTERNATIVE RELAXATION EXERCISE

Sit or lie as comfortably as possible, and close your eyes.
(If during this exercise you experience unusual sensations such as tingling or light-headedness, it is quite normal. If you open your eyes they will go away, and as you carry on with the exercise the feelings will disappear.)

Become aware of your breathing.
Keeping your eyelids closed, screw your eyes up tightly, and relax.
Notice the tiredness in those muscles around your eyes.
Let the warmth of God's healing light relax those muscles further.
Let that feeling of warmth travel to every part of your face, jaw, tongue, neck.
Relax and bathe in God's healing light.
Concentrate on your breathing.

Then let the healing warmth travel slowly down through every part of your body, stopping regularly to pause and concentrate on your breathing.

Allow the healing warmth to relax your shoulders, to travel down your right arm, down through the muscles, down to your finger tips. Do the same with the left arm. Let the relaxation travel down to your chest, your back, and down each leg in turn.
Pause for a few moments.

Go back and concentrate on any part of the body you would like to relax further.

Now concentrate on your favourite relaxing place (real or imagined).
Try and see it in your mind's eye.
Identify the shapes and colours, the sounds, the smells.
Imagine touching something in this peaceful place.
Is Jesus in this place? Is He saying anything to you?
Feel more and more relaxed.

Stay in this place of peace and relaxation until you are ready to return to the room, taking your own time to do this slowly.

APPENDIX 3

EXTRA THOUGHT RECORD PAGE FOR YOUR OWN USE

THOUGHT RECORD

Trigger	Mood	Self-talk/images

Evidence	New self-talk	Re-rate mood

NOTES

CHAPTER 1

1. *Compact Oxford English Dictionary* (OUP, 1996).
2. *Collins English Dictionary*, (Collins, 1976).

CHAPTER 4

1. *Diagnostic and Statistical Manual of Mental Disorders*, Fourth Edition. Primary Care Version (DSM-IV-PC). (American Psychiatric Association, 1995).
2. *Compact Oxford English Dictionary*, op. cit.
3. *Diagnostic and Statistical Manual,* op. cit.

CHAPTER 5

1. Dave Bilbrough © 1987 Kingsway's Thankyou Music.
2. J. John and Mark Stibbe, *A Barrel of Fun* (London: Monarch Books, 2003).
3. Quoted in J. John and Mark Stibbe, *A Box of Delights* (London: Monarch Books, 2001).
4. John Bunyan, *The Pilgrim's Progress* (Oxford World's Classics: Oxford University Press, 2003).
5. J.G. Whittier 1807–92.

FURTHER READING

Baker R., *Understanding Panic Attacks and Overcoming Fear* (Oxford: Lion Publishing, 1995).

Beck A.T., *Anxiety Disorders and Phobias: A Cognitive Perspective* (New York: Basic Books, 1985).

Benson H., *Beyond the Relaxation Response* (New York: Times Books, 1984).

Gittelman R., *Anxiety Disorders of Childhood* (New York: Guildford Press, 1986).

Kennerley Helen, *Overcoming Anxiety: A self-help guide using Cognitive Behaviour Techniques* (London: Constable and Robinson, 1997).

Last C.G. and Hersen M., *Handbook of Anxiety Disorders* (New York: Pergamon Press, 1987).

Lawson Michael, *Facing Anxiety and Stress*, (London: Hodder & Stoughton, 1986).

Mitchell R., *Phobias* (Harmondsworth: Penguin Books, 1982).

Sharpe Robert, *Self-help for your Anxiety*, (London: Souvenir Press, 1997).

Spielberger C., *Understanding Stress and Anxiety* (New York: Harper & Row, 1979).

Wilson R.R., *Don't Panic: Taking Control of Anxiety Attacks* (London: HarperCollins, 1986).

National Distributors

UK: (and countries not listed below)
CWR, Waverley Abbey House, Waverley Lane, Farnham, Surrey GU9 8EP.
Tel: (01252) 784700 Outside UK (44) 1252 784700

AUSTRALIA: CMC Australasia, PO Box 519, Belmont, Victoria 3216.
Tel: (03) 5241 3288 Fax: (03) 5241 3290

CANADA: Cook Communications Ministries, PO Box 98, 55 Woodslee Avenue, Paris, Ontario N3L 3E5.
Tel: 1800 263 2664

GHANA: Challenge Enterprises of Ghana, PO Box 5723, Accra.
Tel: (021) 222437/223249 Fax: (021) 226227

HONG KONG: Cross Communications Ltd, 1/F, 562A Nathan Road, Kowloon.
Tel: 2780 1188 Fax: 2770 6229

INDIA: Crystal Communications, 10-3-18/4/1, East Marredpalli, Secunderabad – 500026, Andhra Pradesh
Tel/Fax: (040) 27737145

KENYA: Keswick Books and Gifts Ltd, PO Box 10242, Nairobi. Tel: (02) 331692/226047
Fax: (02) 728557

MALAYSIA: Salvation Book Centre (M) Sdn Bhd, 23 Jalan SS 2/64, 47300 Petaling Jaya, Selangor.
Tel: (03) 78766411/78766797 Fax: (03) 78757066/78756360

NEW ZEALAND: CMC Australasia, PO Box 303298, North Harbour, Auckland 0751.
Tel: 0800 449 408 Fax: 0800 449 049

NIGERIA: FBFM, Helen Baugh House, 96 St Finbarr's College Road, Akoka, Lagos.
Tel: (01) 7747429/4700218/825775/827264

PHILIPPINES: OMF Literature Inc, 776 Boni Avenue, Mandaluyong City.
Tel: (02) 531 2183 Fax: (02) 531 1960

SOUTH AFRICA: Struik Christian Books, 80 MacKenzie Street, PO Box 1144, Cape Town 8000.
Tel: (021) 462 4360 Fax: (021) 461 3612

SRI LANKA: Christombu Publications (Pvt) Ltd, Bartleet House, 65 Braybrooke Place, Colombo 2.
Tel: (9411) 2421073/2447665

TANZANIA: CLC Christian Book Centre, PO Box 1384, Mkwepu Street, Dar es Salaam.
Tel/Fax: (022) 2119439

USA: Cook Communications Ministries, PO Box 98, 55 Woodslee Avenue, Paris, Ontario N3L 3E5, Canada.
Tel: 1800 263 2664

ZIMBABWE: Word of Life Books (Pvt) Ltd, Christian Media Centre, 8 Aberdeen Road, Avondale,
PO Box A480 Avondale, Harare. Tel: (04) 333355 or 091301188

For email addresses, visit the CWR website: www.cwr.org.uk

CWR is a registered charity – Number 294387

CWR is a limited company registered in England – Registration Number 1990308

Waverley Abbey Insight Series: Insight into Anger

This is a book about anger management: it discusses the topic and provides ways to deal with the potentially life-wrecking state of excessive anger. Full of deep teaching, it takes a practical approach and is packed with valuable case-studies and biblical references.

ISBN: 978-1-85345-437-0
£7.50 (plus p&p)

Other titles available in the Waverley Abbey Insight Series

Insight into Eating Disorders
Helena Wilkinson

An eating disorder is like an iceberg, with the visible tip of symptoms dwarfed by the pain below the surface. Helena Wilkinson, who herself suffered from anorexia as a teenager, examines this complex subject – and gives help in thawing out the iceberg.

ISBN-13: 978-1-85345-410-3
ISBN-10: 1-85345-410-9
£7.50 (plus p&p)

Insight into Self-Esteem
Chris Ledger and Wendy Bray

An honest and personal approach to the problems of low self-esteem. Cultivating healthy self-esteem grows from a deepening relationship with God. The insights shared here incorporate a foundation of established research and a wealth of practical experience.

ISBN-13: 978-1-85345-409-7
ISBN-10: 1-85345-409-5
£7.50 (plus p&p)

Insight into Bereavement
Wendy Bray and
Diana Priest

Bereavements follow a similar path of loss, disbelief, grief and adaptation. This book provides sound advice on coping, whether the bereavement is of a loved one, a marriage or a livelihood. It looks at the effects of loss and at being a channel of God's love to the bereaved.

ISBN-13: 978-1-85345-385-4
ISBN-10: 1-85345-385-4
£7.50 (plus p&p)

Insight into Stress
Beverley Shepherd

An examination of the basics of stress, this book provides practical help and advice on this complex subject. Topics covered include how stress arises, recognising warning signs and coping with the demands and expectations of ourselves and others.

ISBN-13: 978-1-85345-384-7
ISBN-10: 1-85345-384-6
£7.50 (plus p&p)

Prices correct at time of printing